D

EYE-DEEP IN HELL

John Ellis was educated at Blackburn Grammar School,
Sussex University and Manchester University, and now works
as a computer programmer. His previous books include
Armies in Revolution (1973), *A Short History of Guerilla
Warfare* (1975) and *A Short History of the Machine-Gun*
(1976). He is now working on a social history of the British
and American forces in the Second World War.

EYE~DEEP IN HELL

John Ellis

FONTANA/COLLINS

PICTURE CREDITS

Rijksinstituut voor Oorlogsdocumentatie

Pages: 1, 4, 5, 9, 20, 21, 40, 43, 44, 47, 50, 64, 86, 94, 96, 107, 137, 139, 140, 146, 182, 191

John MacClancy
Pages: 4 (bottom), 15, 16, 23, 25, 26 29, 30, 39, 42, 48, 54, 56, 59, 60, 62, 66, 68, 72, 73, 74, 75, 77, 78, 79, 81, 82, 85, 88, 90, 95, 99, 101, 103, 108, 110, 111, 115, 117, 120, 125, 126, 131, 135, 138, 148, 149, 157, 159, 165, 169, 177, 188, 192, 193, 194, 195, 197, 205

Documentation Française
Pages: 11, 37

Australian War Memorial
Pages: 14, 32, 69, 113, 128, 152, 201

David Croom
Pages: 41, 46, 49, 61, 83, 97, 105, 184, 199

Imperial War Museum
Pages: 34 (top), 67, 143, 144, 155, 163, 171, 178, 203

Manchester Public Library
Pages: 53, 55, 76, 130, 150, 175, 186

US National Archives
Pages: 87

John Ellis
Pages: 16, 34, 35, 92, 132, 174, 189

First published by Croom Helm Ltd 1976
First published in Fontana 1977
Copyright © John Ellis 1976

Made and printed in Great Britain by
William Collins Sons & Co. Ltd, Glasgow

Contents

In many acts and quiet observances
You absorbed me:
Until one day I stood eminent
And I saw you gathered round me,
Uplooking,
And about you a radiance that seemed to beat
With variant glow and to give
Grace to our unity.

But, God! I know that I'll stand
Someday in the loneliest wilderness,
Someday my heart will cry
For the soul that has been, but that now
Is scatter'd with the winds,
Deceased and devoid.

I know that I'll wander with a cry;
'O beautiful men, O men I loved,
O whither are you gone, my company?'

War was return of earth to ugly earth,
War was foundering of sublimities,
Extinction of each happy art and faith
By which the world had still kept head in air,
Protesting logic or protesting love,
Until the unendurable moment struck –
The inward scream, the duty to run mad.

Robert Graves

Herbert Read

Prologue

The first weeks of the First World War in August and September 1914 gave a deceptive impression that the campaign was to be a war of movement. For both the Germans and the French, the initial deployments and timetables were based upon the notion of a vast, swift and decisive offensive. In Germany the troop trains and the huge columns of marching men moved according to the dictates of the Schlieffen Plan, by which the French were to be encircled and crushed by German armies moving through Belgium. For the French, the crucial action of the war was to be a massive offensive all along the frontier with Germany – Plan XVII – though 'Plan' is a rather grandiose word for what was little more than a blind faith in the offensive capabilities of the French soldiers. J.F.C. Fuller has described the tactical doctrines of the French General Staff of this time as 'a school of thought rivalled only by the Dervishes of the Sudan'.

The French offensive was an unmitigated disaster. The French generals had underestimated both the number of German divisions available and the devastating firepower that each one possessed. The French infantrymen were mown down in their thousands and any hope of a Christmas vacation in Berlin had to be swiftly abandoned. Nor were German expectations of an early victory march through Paris much nearer the mark. Though the Schlieffen Plan was based upon somewhat more realistic premises, it too began to fall sadly behind schedule. Due partly to the strength of French firepower, and partly to a series of German blunders, the German push ground to a halt. The decisive act was the Battle of the Marne, from 5 to 12 September, after which the whole of the German line began to fall back.

But at least during this period, and during the so-called 'Race to the Sea', lasting until mid-October as each side desperately tried to outflank the others' lines, the war had retained some degree of mobility. The continual marches, the movement of reserves from one sector to another, the clash of

The opening moves: German infantry advancing across open country to attack the French positions in the Lorraine.

Stalemate: British soldiers still dug in three years later at Zillebecke.

skirmishers and cavalry screens, the headlong infantry assaults, all these composed the kind of warfare which each side had envisioned. In the first weeks it seemed possible to believe that war could still be fought according to the precepts of Frederick the Great, Napoleon or von Moltke. Yet by the end of October 1914 the whole battle line in Belgium and France had congealed. The futility of head-on infantry assaults in the face of modern rifles, machine guns and artillery was made apparent. Both sides were forced to dig deep holes in the ground and concentrate upon breaking up any attacks launched by their adversaries.

The armies remained in these holes for the next four years, millions of men trapped in a desolate strip of territory, living and dying in a wilderness of trenches, dugouts, craters, shattered villages and forests of lifeless tree-stumps, a desert in the midst of civilisation, that became more featureless with each passing day. This book is concerned with the way men lived in this physical and spiritual desert. It will show how even in the midst of previously inconceivable conditions, men were able to formulate routines, rules and codes of conduct that could create some kind of order, some kind of meaning in the midst of Chaos itself. For all were agreed that they lived on the very threshold of Hell.

A French infantry lieutenant, Alfred Joubaire, wrote in his diary shortly before he was killed: 'Humanity is mad! It must be mad to do what it is doing. What a massacre! What scenes of horror and carnage! I cannot find words to translate my impressions. Hell cannot be so terrible. Men are mad!' Yet most men lived through the experience and remained more or less sane. Perhaps by examining the nature of that experience, at its most mundane, day-to-day level, it may be possible to discover just how the troops in the trenches managed to discern a necessary and logical reality that enabled them to survive and fight on.

A foretaste of the trenches: German infantry dig rifle pits, 1914.

PART ONE

In the Line

1 The Setting

No pen or drawing can convey this country – the normal setting of the battles taking place day and night, month after month. Evil and the incarnate fiend alone can be master of this war, and no glimmer of God's hand is seen anywhere. Sunset and sunrise are blasphemous, they are mockeries to man, only the black rain out of the bruised and swollen clouds all through the bitter black of night is fit atmosphere in such a land. The rain drives on, the stinking mud becomes evilly yellow, the shell-holes fill up with green-white water, the roads and tracks are covered in inches of slime, the black dying trees ooze and sweat and the shells never cease. They alone plunge overhead, tearing away the rotting tree stumps…annihilating maiming, maddening, they plunge into the grave which is this land; one huge grave, and cast upon it the poor dead. It is unspeakable, godless, hopeless.

Paul Nash

From the very beginning of the war troops on all sides had been forced at times to dig in to obtain some kind of cover against enemy firepower. But the first earthworks they threw up were purely temporary, shallow depressions similar to the slit-trenches and fox-holes of the Second World War. They

A German officer supervises his men digging a trench in the Argonne, 1915.

9

were only to give some minimal protection, for twenty-four hours at the most, prior to moving forwards. But after the Battle of the Marne, when the retreating Germans reached the Aisne, General von Falkenhayn decided that his troops must at all costs hold on to those parts of France and Belgium that they still occupied. The Germans he felt, could afford to sit tight and hold off any attacks that the Allies, particularly the French, would be obliged to launch. They were the ones who had to liberate their country from the invader; therefore let them break themselves upon a well-fortified German defensive line. So the Germans dug in, intending to remain just where they were. The Allies soon found that they were incapable of breaking through this line and they too began to create a permanent line of earthworks. It was never conceived of as more than a jumping-off point for an ultimately decisive breakthrough, but even the most obtuse Allied commander realised that their forces might have to remain where they were for quite a few months.

The beginning of trench warfare proper is usually given as September 1914, when the German VII Reserve Corps turned around on the Chemin des Dames Ridge and blocked th advance of the British I Corps. Within a few weeks the stalemate that occurred there had spread down the whole battle-line. This line spread from the North Sea to the Swiss Frontier. Obviously, on such a long line, 475 miles in all, the nature of the terrain varied considerably, and this in turn had its effect upon the type of trenches and fortifications that were built. The northern part of the front, in Belgium and in France as far south as the Somme, was held by the British. Here was to be found some of the worst terrain of all and conditions in the British trenches were often nightmarish.

The line began at Nieuport on the coast and then ran along the flooded Yser to Dixmude. From there it ran around the notorious Ypres Salient and across the French frontier north-west of Armentières. This Flanders countryside was very flat and rarely more than a metre or two above sea level. The nearest English equivalent would be the fenlands of Cambridgeshire and Lincolnshire. In such conditions the most trivial little bump in the ground, never more than sixty metres above sea level, became an important strategic point. Unfortunately most of them were held by the Germans. Having been the first to decide to stand fast and dig they had always been able to choose the most advantageous spots. Two of the most important were Hill 60, two miles south-west of Ypres, and the Wytschaete-Messines Ridge, a little to the south.

Not only did possession of the higher ground give the Germans a tactical advantage, but it also forced the British to live in the foulest conditions. As soon as they began to dig down they would invariably find water two or three feet below

NORTH
SEA

HOLLAND

R. Waal

R. Maas

BELGIUM

Antwerp

Brussels

GERMANY

Cologne

Aix-la-Chapelle

Zeebrugge

Ostend

Dunkirk

Ghent

R. Schelde

Liège

Namur

R. Meuse

Huy

Mons

Charleroi

R. Yser

JULY 1917

JUNE 1917

Passchendaele

Ypres

Menin

Messines

Bailleul

Armentières

St. Omer

Hazebrouck

Lille

Lillers

MAR. 1915

Neuve Chapelle

La Bassée

Béthune

Loos

SEPT. 1915

Lens

St. Pol

APRIL 1917

VIMY RIDGE

Douai

ARTOIS

Arras

APRIL 1917

Doullens

Cambrai

Bapaume

JULY 1916

Albert

Péronne

Amiens

JULY 1916

St. Quentin

Somme

PICARDY

Montdidier

Lassigny

Noyon

Compiègne

R. Oise

Senlis

Chantilly

Soissons

APRIL 1917

APRIL 1917

R. Ourcq

Château Thierry

R. Oise

Ham

La Fère

Laon

R. Aisne

Reims

APRIL 1917

Epernay

R. Marne

Châlons

Pt. Morin

Gd. Morin

MARSHES OF ST. GOND

R. Seine

Paris

CHAMPAGNE

Valenciennes

Maubeuge

R. Escaut

R. Sambre

Le Câteau

Guise

Givet

ARDENNES

Neufchâteau

Mézières

Sedan

Luxembourg

Virton

R. Meuse

Longuyon

FEB. 1916

Briey

FEB. 1916

Verdun

FOREST OF ARGONNE

St. Mihiel

Bar le Duc

R. Ornain

R. Marne

Toul

LORRAINE

Metz

Morhange

R. Moselle

Thionville

R. Saar

Saarburg

Trier

R. Moselle

Nancy

R. Meurthe

Charmes

Epinal

VOSGES

ALSACE

Belfort

R. Rhine

R. Meuse

N

WESTERN FRONT

—·—·—·— Approximate line at end of 1914

○○○○○○○○ Line at end of Hindenburg Retreat, February 1917

━━━━━━ Line on 11th Nov. 1918

0   50

Miles

the surface. Along the whole line, from the coast to La Bassée, trench life involved a never-ending struggle against water and mud. Around Nieuport the terrain was little more than one big flood, the tide only being controlled by a complex series of locks, dams and canals. Trenches proper were quite out of the question and the British front was a series of sandbag breastworks and fortified islands. The Germans did their best to make life even more intolerable by continually shelling the locks and trying to flood out the defenders. In the rest of Flanders the British were soon forced to give up the unequal struggle against the mud and the constantly collapsing trenches. From January 1915 they took to constructing what were called parapet or command trenches. The Germans referred to them as box trenches. In these one only dug down, if at all, to a maximum of one or two feet and the rest of the trench was built up with thick walls of sandbags. These latter were rarely filled with sand; earth or, best of all, clay was generally used. Such trenches were usually between seven and eight feet deep and six to seven feet wide. The walls of sandbags themselves were made as thick as possible to absorb any bullets or shell fragments. Often they measured as much as ten feet at the top and twenty feet at the base. In certain parts of the line the ground was too swampy to permit even the creation of secure command trenches. In the La Bassée sector, which lay below sea level, a system of ferro-concrete emplacements had to be built. The 42nd East Lancashire Division on one Brigade front of about 2,000 yards used 5,036 bags of cement, 19,384 bags of shingle and 9,692 bags of sand in creating a single reserve trench line. Even excluding the necessary water, this involves over 900 tons of materials, most of which had to be manhandled by those members of the Division not actually in the fire trenches.

There was one other sector of the line in which command trenches were standard practice. This was in the Argonne, held by the French, where again it was found that the water level was much too near the surface. In all other areas the troops simply dug themselves a deep hole in the ground. But whether trenches were dug or built, they were all – French, German or British – designed according to the same basic pattern. In the fenland of Flanders, the slagheaps of industrial Artois, the chalky downlands of Picardy, the marshy lowlands of the Somme Valley, along the line of the Aisne, through Champagne, the Argonne, Lorraine and across the mountainous Vosges, each side created for themselves fairly uniform defence systems, and relearnt a vocabulary that owed more to Vauban than to the theories of contemporary military science.

The front of the trench was known as the parapet, generally abut ten feet high. Even in trenches which were dug down, the top two or three feet of the parapet would consist of a thick

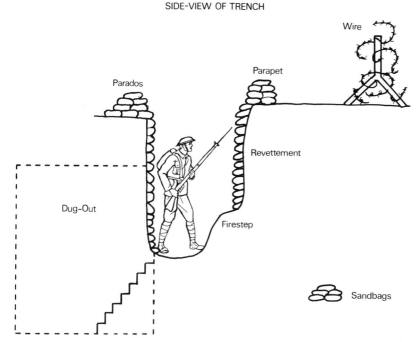

line of sandbags. Obviously, in a trench of this depth it would be impossible to see or fire over the top, so there was built at the bottom a two or three-foot high ledge known as the fire-step. This was used by those on sentry duty, or by the whole unit when 'standing to' to face a possible enemy attack. The back wall of the trench was known as the parados, and it too was often built up with sandbags. Except in a particularly favourable terrain, notably chalk, it was not possible to expect the sides of a trench to stand up of their own accord. Rainfall, natural pressures and shell-fire would inevitably cause extensive subsidences. To minimise the chance of such disasters it was usual to revet the parapet and parados. The British and Germans generally used sandbags and timber, whilst the French were more inclined to use hurdles, bunches

French troops standing to on the fire-step of their trench. Note the typically French wattle revettements.

of twigs and branches cut from surrounding trees. Stone was rarely used, partly because of the effort involved in transporting it, but also because it was unwise to build a revetment too solidly. The French had tried using stone in trenches near Compiègne and it was found that, whilst the parapet did not collapse, the weight of the trapped rainwater simply pushed the sides of the trenches closer and closer together.

Of course trenches were not simply long, straight lines. This would have presented terrible dangers should the enemy ever have broken into the trench line. Then they could have simply set up a machine gun and fired right down the trench (i.e. enfiladed fire). Thus the trench was broken up into small sections, each screened from the other by a barrier of earth and sandbags jutting out into the trench. The straight sections, perhaps ten yards long, were known as firebays, where the infantryman usually stood when on duty or alert, whilst the 'kinks' in the line were known as traverses. Seen from the air a trench line had the crenellated appearance of the battlements on a castle. The Germans adopted an identical system, though the French were inclined to do without the laborious chain or bays and traverses, preferring instead a simple zig-zag line. One British officer described his misgivings on moving into a trench previously occupied by a French unit:

An almost too perfect example of a sand-bagged trench showing the traverses and firebays.

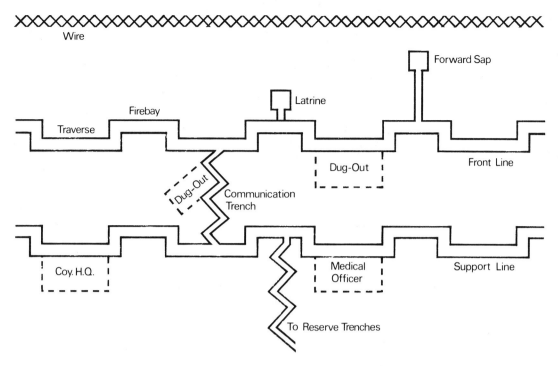

While the parapet was non-existent, an enormous mound of earth . . . the parados, rose behind our heads. Then, instead of being traversed by great bulkheads of sandbags, there was no protection at all at the sides of the bays. An occasional fascine stood, like a stone vase in some noble parterre, to give decoration to a dull alley.

The front-line trench was not, in fact, the most forward defensive position. Running out at right-angles to most trenches were what were known as saps, narrow passages some twenty or thirty yards long leading to an isolated little position for two or three men. These were the listening posts where for a couple of hours at a time the sentries would squat, peering into the darkness and straining to hear the slightest sound from the enemy lines. A French soldier spoke of 'the little listening posts of terrible memory. It is difficult to imagine the suffering of the sentries. . . How often did the absolute solitude provoke panic at the slightest movement of an animal in the grass, at the stirring of a branch in the moonlight?' These listening posts were often in shell craters. In 1916 and 1917, particularly, a shell falling in no man's land would precipitate a series of minor but bloody attacks and counter-attacks as each side tried to seize the new crater and connect it to their own lines with a new sap. For some time it was a General Order that any British unit had to occupy any shell crater created within sixty yards of their line. These were

An aerial view of the Hindenburg line as seen from 8,000 feet.

often consolidated as 'cruciform' posts, formed of two trenches intersecting at right angles.

Trenches also had outlets from the back. For they were usually built in triple lines: the fire trench, the support trench and the reserve trench or dugouts. In the more compicated German systems there might be as many as ten lines of trenches. To allow soldiers to move to the front or rear in comparatively safety communication trenches were built between the various lines. They were usually the same depth and width as ordinary fire trenches but did not have traverses and firebays. But these too were never constructed in a straight line, and went out in a zig-zag. On the British front by 1917 some of these communication trenches were as much as three miles long.

Another indispensable feature of any piece of trench was the dugout, a shelter or burrow to give some sort of protection against the elements and enemy artillery. Oficers could almost always expect to find a corner in some kind of dugout, but the ordinary soldiers, in many cases, had to make do with even cruder refuges. Sometimes they simply spread pieces of wood, corrugated iron or tarpaulin across the trench from parapet to parados. In other cases they would scoop out a hollow in the front or back of the trench. Here, wrapped in their groundsheets, they would snatch their brief periods of sleep, curled up parallel to the trench or with their feet sticking out into it. This system of personal 'funk-holes' was particularly common among the French. In the German and English lines, in theory at least, it was banned because of the increased danger of the trench walls subsiding. Nevertheless, any unit marching along a trench at night would provoke a monotonous series of muffled oaths as they stumbled over the legs of sleeping soldiers.

Dugouts proper varied enormously in size, comfort and security. But this description by a New Zealand officer presents a fairly typical picture:

> Three-quarters of an inch of candle dimly lights up a space too cramped for one man to turn round in comfortably, much less to provide sleeping and living quarters for three ... On a ledge with a sloping board above it on which, if you started up in the night you would strike your head, lies bedding; three waterproof sheets and three greatcoats, no blankets. The remainder of the limited airspace is filled with three sets of equipment . . . The roofing iron is sufficient to keep out the sun, but lets in the rain.

Water could be expected in almost any dugout, along with muddy floors, running walls, low ceilings and a dank and fetid atmosphere. Otherwise they were anything but standardised. In one spot an incoming unit would find nothing more than a ten-foot deep hole, roofed over with five layers of logs. In October 1915 dugouts in front of Kemmel were tiny 'rooms', four foot by seven, containing a bed, six foot by two, and two two-foot square tables made of board and old boxes. The walls and corrugated iron roofs were lined with sandbags and two small holes were made to serve as doorway and window. A company headquarters of the Royal Warwickshire Fusiliers in late 1914 consisted of two rooms, each lined with timber. The amenities inside actually included a tablecloth, a lamp and a homemade set of bookshelves. Charles Carrington has given this description of another company headquarters near Gommecourt Wood in 1917:

> It is an old French dugout scooped out under a bank with hurdles against the earth walls, and a roof reinforced with stout timber and sandbags, giving just room for a very small table made of old boxes, and two bunks made of wire-netting stretched on frames. Opening out of it is a still smaller den, in which an officer's servant is cooking over a charcoal brazier that gives the cave its characteristic smell.

The dugouts so far described were of the kind found in the front-line trenches, and were not generally as deep as those found further back. This might seem surprising at first sight, but the reason is in fact fairly logical. It was unusual for either side to employ their heavy artillery to shell the enemy's front-line trenches because of the danger of a near miss falling on their own lines or dangerously undermining their own trenches. The big guns were usually trained on reserve and rear areas, and it was here that one was obliged to dig deep. Here the men had recourse either to what were known as mine dugouts, some of them thirty or forty feet deep, or else

'The Labyrinth' at Arras —
taken by the British in hand
to hand fighting.

converted cellars in the ruined towns and villages. Around
Arras, for example, the British occupied the *boves*, large
pillared underground chambers, more like a church crypt
than an English cellar. One dugout at Mont Quentin was
actually in a church and was reached by descending a
stairway of forty-seven steps from the vault of the church. In
the village of Roclincourt the cellars were linked up to create
quite extensive dugouts. Some were twenty feet deep, reached
by two separate stairways in case one should be blocked by a
direct hit, and had up to three rooms, as well as bunks for
officers and men. Around Hamel, in a chalky region, the
reserve lines contained deep bunkers, known to the men as
'Kentish villas', which had been tunnelled out by parties of
Kent miners. Even in the front line one occasionally found
mine dugouts. In the Arras sector, for example, in early 1916

there was at least one shelter that was thirty feet deep. Made up of two small rooms, one decorated with pink wallpaper and one with green, it also contained a bed, several easy chairs, a stove, a mantelpiece and a large mirror.

It is generally agreed that the Germans were much better off than the Allies with respect to their dugouts. In the front line there was little difference. One German officer has described the forward trenches in Champagne where the available shelter was nothing more than recesses dug in the chalk walls and covered with boards and a few shovelfuls of soil. Their inherent dampness caused the infantrymen to refer to them as 'drip wells' or 'men's baths'. But further back the accommodation was, under the circumstances, almost lavish. Such was the case in the Somme Valley in 1916. Here the dugouts were thirty or forty feet deep, connected by tunnels and steel railway systems. Electric light and ventilation was provided in all rooms, and many of them had panelled walls and planked floors. An English chaplain who visited some captured German trenches during the Battle of the Somme described the extreme lengths to which the Germans went to make these dugouts habitable. The walls were boarded with neatly morticed timbers, telephone wires were laid along the walls, iron girders were boxed in, ceilings were painted white, woodwork varnished, and in the officers' quarters one even found wooden beading, carpets on the floors and glass windows. The Reverend was probably mistaken about the windows. Another eye-witness pointed out that the German dugouts captured near Le Sars contained 'port holes' of mirrored glass to give the illusion of being able to look out.

British officers in a captured German dugout. Note the wall paper and wooden panelling.

Identical types of dugout were to be found in every part of the German line between Lille and Metz, particularly in the elaborate defensive positions, *Stellungs,* that made up the Hindenburg Line. There were seven of these in all, of which the most famous were the Siegfried Stellung, from Cambrai to St. Quentin, and the Kriemhilde Stellung in the Argonne.

Although the triple concept of forward, reserve and support postions remained basic to each side throughout the war, there were considerable shifts of emphasis as tactics evolved. The most important of these concerned the manning of the front-line trenches. At the beginning of the trench war proper all sides felt it necessary to put a substantial proportion of their available strength into the front line, in the hope of breaking up an enemy attack as it crossed no man's land. But if the enemy did succeed in breaking through, or if he laid down a particularly heavy artillery bombardment on the front line, then one risked losing all the forward troops as prisoners or casualties. There might well then be insufficient reserves available for an effective counter-attack.

A German field telephone in a front line dugout.

At an early stage in the war the French tried to avoid this by dividing the front line into what they called 'active' and 'passive' zones. The former were heavily fortified positions designed to give flanking fire to the passive zones on each side. These latter were very heavily wired but only manned by a few sentries. Behind these was a line of shell-proof strong points to accomodate the support companies. Finally, some two miles to the rear, was a 'stop-line', again divided into active and passive zones, which was meant to be the last line of resistance to any breakthrough. Once Hindenburg had replaced

Falkenhayn as the supreme commander on the Western Front, in 1917, the Germans adopted such a system of defence in depth. Under Falkenhayn they had tended to entrust themselves to a single heavily defended line, with concrete machine gun emplacements a thousand or so yards in the rear. At first many German soldiers were very loathe to adopt any other type of defence. Describing the effort to introduce Hindenburg's new system, the Crown Prince wrote: 'In practice [the troops] clung for a very long while to the traditional habit of building one defensive line in a manner quite inadequate, and it was only with hesitation and reluctance that they resorted to the system of building multiple lines.' But Hindenburg and Ludendorff were determined that habits must change, and within twelve months or so most officers were familiar with the new tactical concepts. This is how Hindenburg himself described them:

> In future our defensive positions were no longer to consist of single lines and strong points but of a network of lines and groups of strong points. In the deep cones thus formed we did not intend to dispose our troops on a rigid and continuous front but in a complex system of nuclei and distributed in breadth and depth. The defender had to keep his forces mobile to avoid the destructive effects of the enemy fire during the period of artillery preparation, as well as to abandon voluntarily any parts of the line which could no longer be held, and then to recover by a counter-attack all the points which were essential to the maintenance of the whole position.

Using primitive periscopes and mirrors British soldiers observe the 'Hun' lines from below the firing line.

An aerial view of no man's land. Note the duck-board road in lower left hand corner.

The British responded to the problem of the overmanning of the front line in a typically haphazard manner. Force of circumstance, rather than systematic planning was the main influence. In the first winter of the war, in Flanders, the front line was merely a thinly held string of individual outposts. There was no opportunity to link these together until the following spring and summer. But in the following three years the local situation often made it impossible to maintain a continuous front line. In the winter of 1915-16, for example, the line in front of Serre was almost untenable because of the effects of the weather. One company's frontage consisted of just thirteen individual outposts. By early 1916 the British line below Vimy Ridge was similarly held because of the German habit of digging under the enemy trenches and detonating large mines. In August 1916 one writer went so far as to say: 'The war of trenches is a comfortable, out-of-date phase, to be looked upon with regret...The war of today is a war of craters and potholes – a war of crannies and nicks, and crevices torn out of the earth yesterday, and to be shattered into new shapes tomorrow.' On the Somme front, in October and November 1916, the appalling weather and tremendous German artillery concentration left units at the front with neither the time nor the opportunity to revet the sides of the battered trenches. The front line was reduced to a series of mud holes and remained that way throughout the winter.

Eventually the British High Command began to react to this new situation. Aware, on the one hand, that local circumstances often made it impossible to maintain a continuous line and, on the other, of the new German theories of trench defence, Headquarters issued a set of instructions to standardise the situation. The trench system was to be modified into three networks of outposts, to be known as the Forward Zone, the Battle Zone and the Rear Zone. In the

Making a trench by joining shell craters.

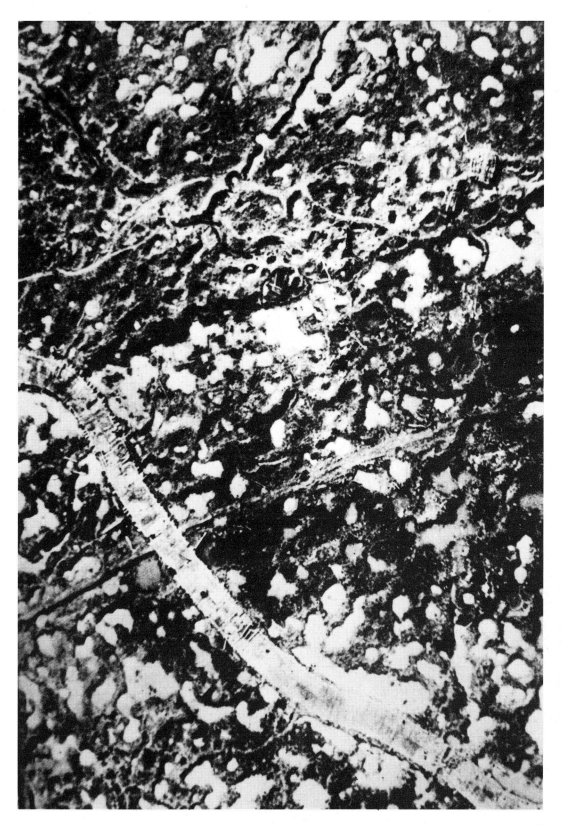

Forward Zone were to be the machine guns and one third of the men. In the Battle Zone, two miles back, were to be two-thirds of the artillery and a third as many men again. The remaining men were to be grouped in the Rear Zone as a mobile reserve. Though largely copied from the German instructions these differed in one crucial respect. The British had left themselves with less than one third of their men as a mobile reserve, whereas in the German lines (and the French) up to two-thirds of the available troops were held back for manoeuvre and counter-attack. The British were to pay the price for this persistent overmanning of the front areas in March 1918 when the great German offensive opened with an artillery barrage that incapacitated a huge proportion of the men in the sector under immediate attack. Indeed, in many areas the reorganisation had not even got under way. It was not until July 1918 that Duff Cooper noted in his diary that the old front line 'held by an unbroken line of soldiers standing in the trenches almost shoulder to shoulder ... had been replaced by a series of strong points divided from one another by as much as four or five hundred yards'.

But what of that narrow strip that divided two opposing trench lines – 'no man's land'? The very negativeness of the concept is testimony to the tactical and strategic bankruptcy that was revealed on the Western Front, whilst it also hints at the utter desolation, at the uselessness of this pulverised, barren vacuum. The width of no man's land varied a great deal from sector to sector. It was usually between ten and five hundred yards, the average distance between the trenches being two to three hundred yards. In Flanders, the average was a little less, probably about 150 yards. But, it is very difficult to generalise. Around Cambrai, one of the easiest British sectors, there was a dead zone of 500 yards; whilst at Les Boeufs, near Guillemont, it was only fifty yards. Sometimes the two sides were almost nose to nose. Near Zonnebeke in 1915 the British and Germans were only seven or eight yards apart, and in certain trenches in La Boisselle it has been claimed that the opposing sentries could have crossed their bayonets. In the Ypres Salient, the worst part of the British lines, the trenches were always very close. At one point the Canadians found themselves at one end of a ruined barn and the Germans at the other. On the Bellewaarde Ridge, in 1915, the British and the Germans actually shared the same front-line trench. All that divided them was a thick barrier of sandbags and barbed wire.

Wire, of course, was a ubiquitous feature of no man's land. One of the most common fatigues for the men in the trenches was the wiring party. Almost every night a little group would have to crawl over their own parapets and repair an old entanglement or add even more. At first the wire was supported with stakes knocked in with padded mallets, but

later someone came up with the idea of giving the stakes a corkscrew tip so that they could be noiselessly inserted into the ground. For obvious reasons the wire was always placed at least a grenade's throw from one's own trench. The amount used varied a great deal, depending largely on the zeal and industriousness of the unit in the line. The Germans were particularly keen in this respect. Their wire was hardly ever less than fifty feet deep, and in many places it was a hundred feet more In the Siegfried Line every trench had at least ten belts of wire in front of it. The French, too, relied heavily on this kind of obstruction. In the Fourth Army trenches near Rheims in April 1916 it was an Army Order that each unit had to add at least two yards to the thickness of the wire every week.

This reliance upon positional defence, created quite unprecedented material demands. The French, for example, at the end of 1915, estimated that there were twenty miles of trench for each mile of the line. By August of the following year the figure was thought to be half as much again. If this figure is accurate, it means that on the Allied side, on the entire Western Front, there were some 15,000 miles of trenches! It is not surprising, therefore that whilst the normal annual provision of shovels and spades for the British Army, before 1914, was 2,500, from August 1914 to the end of the war, on all fronts, 10,638,000 were provided.

2 The Daily Routine

Just as the exact configurations of the trenches varied a great deal from sector to sector and from year to year, so did the daily timetables which the men followed whilst they were in the line. No unit, from platoon to corps, ever spent the whole of its time in the trenches. At more or less regular intervals the individual soldier could expect to be pulled out of the line, either to be placed in reserve or sent to a rest camp. Germans, French, Americans and British all followed the basic sequence of service in the line, a spell in reserve and a much shorter period of rest. But the length and frequency of these periods varied enormously. An obstacle to any lucid summary of the routine of trench life is the vague usage of the terms 'in the line' or 'up', in 'support', in 'reserve' or 'resting'. The exact significance of these terms depends upon the size of the unit being referred to. Thus, if just two companies are referred to as being 'in support', this will mean that they are directly behind the first-line trench, which will be occupied by another company of their battalion. But if a whole battalion is spoken of as being 'in support', this will mean that it is just behind the whole complex of the forward trenches. Similarly, a company or a platoon that is 'up' will be in the fire trench, whilst a battalion that is 'up' will be between the various lines of trenches and village dugouts that make up the forward zone as a whole. The words 'reserve' and 'rest' are equally ambiguous. A company in reserve might simply be in the third line of forward trenches. But often whole divisions, even corps, would be taken out of the line. A division resting thus would be about fifteen miles behind the lines, whereas a corps could be fifty miles away.

The following summary by a British officer who served in France gives as clear a picture as any of the routine followed by a battalion in the forward positions:

The division held a front of about four miles as the bullet flies, much longer following the trace of the trenches. All three brigades were in the line, side by side, each with two battalions 'up', one in close support and one back in reserve ... 'resting', which meant that six battalions out of thirteen [the thirteenth was a pioneer battalion] in the division held the line. Each of these front-line battalions would normally have two of its companies 'up', and two held back in supporting positions ... In my battalion, the 5th Royal Warwickshires ... each company had three platoons actually posted in the front trenches, and one standing to arms as an 'inlying picket' under cover, ready to act in any emergency at two or three minutes' notice. If this may be taken as typical...the six front-line battalions at quiet times held the whole divisional front with about thirty-six platoon posts, and since a platoon could rarely put more than thirty men on duty, we may conclude that the divisional front was held by 1,000 of its, say, 10,000 infantrymen.

The Seaforths snatch a moment's rest in a front line trench.

In other divisions the arrangement differed in detail. In the 60th Division in 1916 only two brigades were actually in the line, the other being held back in reserve. In late 1917 when divisions were reduced from thirteen to ten battalions, there were only three battalions per brigade: two in the line and one out. Battalion routine also varied in the disposition of companies. In late 1914, all four companies of a battalion often occupied the line, there not being sufficient reserves available to work out a rotation system. Whereas in later years it was common for only two or three companies to be in the line with the remaining men held in reserve.

Nor was there any standardisation of the time a unit might spend at any one point in the sequence. In August 1915, at Hébuterne, a battalion spent eight days in the line and four in reserve. On the Somme, in the winter of 1915-16, a battalion could expect to make two eight-day tours of duty in the line, one in support and one at rest. On Kemmel Hill in 1915, battalions had to spend six days in the line and only two in reserve. The usual German procedure at this time was four days in the line, two in support and four at rest.

In times of crisis the time spent in the line, and in the fire trenches themselves, was often much longer. In December 1914 at Le Touquet, the medical officer of the 2nd Battalion Lancashire Fusiliers had recommended that it was unwise for men to spend more than forty-eight hours at a time in the actual trenches. But in Flanders, at this time, one Scottish battalion spent thirty-eight consecutive days in the line. In 1915, a battalion of the West Yorkshires did one of the most gruelling tours of all, in the Loos Salient, when they spent seventy out of ninety days in the trenches. Things did not improve in the following year. In February at Hébuterne the 1st Battalion of the 5th Royal Warwickshires spent twenty-eight continuous days at the front. During the Battle of the Somme it was quite common for battalions to spend two or three weeks in the line, and one, the 13th Yorkshire and Lancashire, was there for an incredible fifty-one consecutive days.

The experience of a typical regimental officer gives some impression of the amount of time an individual soldier might expect to be in the trenches. Between December 1914 and August 1916 Colonel Jack of the 1st Cameronians spent 141 days in the trenches, ninety days in Brigade Support, twenty-three days in Brigade Reserve, ninety-seven days in Divisional Reserve, seventeen days in Army Reserve, fifteen days moving from sector to sector, nineteen days in hospital and twelve days on leave. In crude terms one might express this as 231 days in danger of being killed or wounded as against 183 days of comparative safety. Charles Carrington, an officer in the Royal Warwickshires, has made his own analysis of his diary for 1916:

I find that ... I spent 65 days in the front line trenches, and 36 more in supporting positions close at hand ... In addition 120 days were spent in reserve positions near enough to the line to march up for the day when work or fighting demanded, and 73 days were spent out in rest ... 10 days were spent in Hospital ... 17 days ... on leave ... and days travelling ... The 101 days under fire contain twelve 'tours' in the trenches varying in length from one to thirteen days. The battalion made sixteen in all during the year ... We were in action four times during my ... tours in the trenches. Once I took part in a direct attack, twice in bombing actions, and once we held the front line from

London omnibuses used to rush troops to the front.

which other troops advanced. I also took part in an unsuccessful trench raid.

The interesting point here is that attacks and offensives were rare. In fact they formed very small portion of the soldier's active service. Whilst in the trenches, troops on both sides only saw the enemy very infrequently. Carrington, for example, in three tours in the forward trenches, in November and December 1916 never saw a German, even though his battalion suffered fifty battle casualties. Another officer, Captain Greenwell of the 4th Oxfordshire & Bucks Light Infantry, arrived at the front in late May 1915, but he did not see his first German until the 3rd of August.

A final point to be made about this rota of trench service is that soldiers rarely found themselves in the same place more than three or four times. A British soldier in France for more than a few months could expect to serve in three, four or five quite different sectors. Moreover, even in the same sector, he would be continually moving from trenches to billets, back to new trenches and then to fresh billets. Carrington has estimated that, in 1916 he had to move all his equipment eighty times; fourteen of these by rail and sixty-six on a route march. Jack was equally peripatetic. He found himself in twenty different trench positions and was billeted in nineteen towns and villages.

This is one of the few respects in which German trench routine was much different from that of the British. German regiments tended to remain much longer in one place. Ernst Jünger, of the 73rd Hanoverian Fusilier Regiment, for example, spent eighteen months in the same small part of the line, near Douchy, in Artois. One German unit, on Vimy Ridge, the Bavarian 1st Reserve Division, which faced the Canadian assault in April 1917, had been there almost from the beginning of the war. Similarly, when the Americans attacked the Kriemhilde Stellung in 1918, they found themselves opposed by whole divisions which had been in that sector since 1914. In 1914 and 1915, German units also had less chance to alternate within their particular sector. As the Crown Prince put it: 'We did not enjoy the invaluable advantages [in terms of numbers] of our enemies, who were able to make good the wear and tear of nerve strength by frequent reliefs and periods of rest.' Only at Verdun in 1916, did the Germans manage to take divisions out of the line after only a few days, and even then they had to be placed elsewhere in the line, though this time in a quieter sector.

But, as far as possible, the Germans also tried to follow the same basic sequence of trenches, support and reserve *cum* rest. Where possible again, the duration of each of these periods was limited to from four to seven days. The same is true of the French who, on average, could expect to alternate four-day

stretches in the trenches with four days in billets. After three or four trench tours they would then be pulled into the reserve for a few days. In the quieter, southern sectors, these periods would be much longer. In the Vosges, for example, a soldier might be in the line for three weeks before being pulled back for a ten to fourteen-day rest. Like the British, the French also moved regularly, by division, from sector to sector.

Staff officer from GHQ (note arm band) studying details before the opening of the British offensive. The company's rum ration is securely tied up in the left hand corner of the dugout.

In the Front Line

The company would take up its new position after at least one night in billets, which they had reached, as like as not, by a route march from another part of the sector. These in themselves were gruelling experiences, the troops often covering fifteen or twenty miles. Only ten minutes rest was allowed every hour, and in summer the exertion often proved too much. A Coldstream Guards' officer, Lieutenant St. Leger, described one such march in which many men fell out, fainted or had fits. Once his battalion reached billets it was decreed that everyone who had fallen out had to do a further five hours route marching in full kit; those who had not actually been unconscious at the time also had to suffer eight days CB (confined to barracks).

Walking knee deep in mud along a communication trench. The photograph fairly illustrates the conditions of the trenches in low lying areas during the winter months.

The men would move up to the front line at night, because of the threat of hostile artillery. Most of the journey would be through the communication trenches, each platoon being separated by intervals of a hundred yards, again in deference to the enemy artillery. This journey in itself could be an exhausting experience. There was no light and each man could only stumble along after the person in front of him, often through inches of mud or water. A.P. Herbert remembered such a trip up to the front line:

> When at last we came into the deep communication trench we felt that the end of [our] weariness must surely be near. But the worst exasperations of relieving an unknown line were still before us. It was a two-mile trudge in the narrow ditches to the front line. No war correspondent has ever described such a march; it is not included in the official 'horrors of war'; but this is the kind of thing, more than battle or blood which harasses the spirit of the infantryman and composes his life…Each man [becomes] a mere lifeless automaton … Mechanically each man grapples with the obstacles, mechanically repeats the ceaseless messages that are passed up and down … to those behind, and stumbles on. He is only conscious of the dead weight of his load, and the braces of his pack biting into his shoulders, of his thirst and the sweat of his body, and the longing to lie down and sleep. When we halt men fall into a doze as they stand and curse pitifully when they are urged on from behind.

And that in a dry trench network in Gallipoli. If one also adds the additional burden of dragging one's feet, with every step, out of the mud, one can begin to imagine the utter exhaustion of going up the line in France or Flanders.

Whether on the march or picking his way up the communication trench, each soldier carried his pack and equipment with him. The actual weight of the infantryman's equipment varied with the season, and whether one was on the march or not. The average weight of a British private's accoutrements was about 60 lbs, though in winter the norm was about 77 lbs. The Official History points out that it is a well-known fact that the optimum weight for a man to carry is one third of his own weight. On average, a British recruit weighed 132 lbs and was therefore consistently grossly overloaded. Estimations of the weight of the German equipment vary between 55 to over 100 lbs, though the latter figure was a rare occurrence whilst on the march, and the average was around 70 lbs. The French infantryman's load was as much as 85 lbs, an awesome figure no matter how well it might be distributed. This equipment comprised of: two blankets rolled up in a groundsheet, a spare pair of boots, a sheepskin or quilted coat, a shovel or pair of heavy

Typical British troops on the Western front. In winter his equipment often weighed as much as 77 lbs.

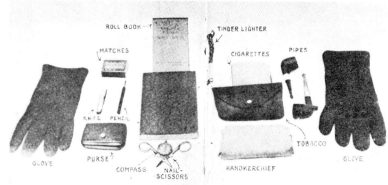

ROLL BOOK

MATCHES

TINDER LIGHTER

CIGARETTES   PIPES

KNIFE PENCIL

PURSE

COMPASS NAIL-
SCISSORS

GLOVE

TOBACCO

HANDKERCHIEF

GLOVE

KNIFE, FORK, SPOON,
AND MUG.

GROCERY RATIONS

BISCUIT

MEAT
LOZENGES

BISCUIT

GROCERY RATION

BULLY BEEF

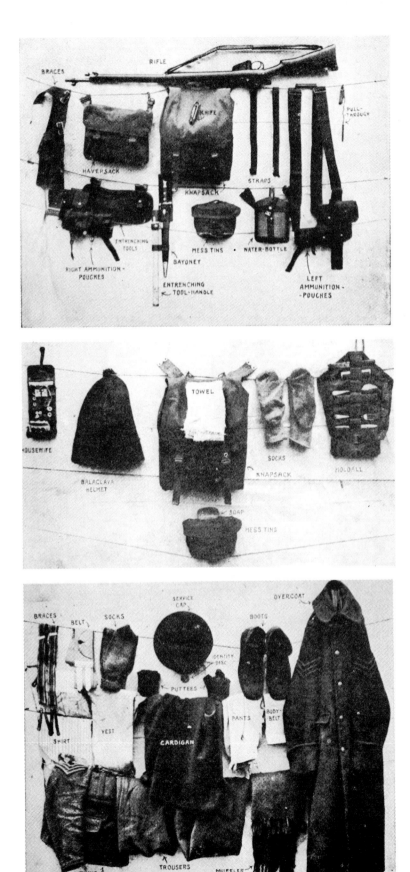

wire-clippers, a mess-tin and a large pail for rations, two litres of wine, two quarts of water, food for four days, 200 cartridges, six hand grenades and a gas-mask, as well as assorted clothes and personal belongings. The whole lot was carried in an interlaced harness known as a *barda*, usually referred to as the 'bazaar' or more often the 'bordello'. The knapsack itself was referred to as 'Azor', the French equivalent of 'Fido', because at the beginning of the war it was made of dogskin.

Robert Graves has given a list of the minimum equipment of the British soldier, often added to by tools, extra weapons or personal souvenirs.

Great coat	Towel
Mess-tin	Housewife
Shirt	Holdall
Socks (3 pairs)	Razor and case
Soap	Latherbrush
Comb	Waterproof sheet
Knife, fork and spoon	Tin of grease
Toothbrush	Field-dressing
Cardigan	Gas-mask
Cap comforter	Spine protector
Paybook	Set of equipment
Ammunition (150 rounds)	Bootlaces
Rifle cover	Rifle and bayonet
Bottle of oil	Entrenching tool
Water bottle	Pull-through

British officers were limited to 45 lbs of personal luggage, though they did not have to carry this about with them. It went with the battalion transport. German equipment was almost identical, though they also carried a pair of drawers, a pair of 'slacks' and an extra shirt, as well as the wherewithal to construct half a tent. Again the whole set of equipment was arranged in a harness, that could be taken on and off like an overcoat.

The infantryman was equally burdened down at head and foot. His boots each weighed about five pounds. Nor, in the British Army at least, were these boots of particularly good quality. If they did not fit a man was doomed to endless agonies because the leather uppers had no stretch in them – that is of course if the boots did not disintegrate first. All through April 1916, the 42nd East Lancashire Division had a substantial percentage of men confined to barracks because they were awaiting new boots. The 2nd Battalion of the Buffs were issued with new boots in England in early 1915. The heels soon fell off most of them and the nails came through. As the regimental historian noted: 'Someone was to blame, of course, presumably the contractor, and it seems that in every war these men must make their fortunes at the expense of the soldier.' In 1914 all sides had worn soft headgear of some kind. The British helmet was introduced in February 1916, though at first it was issued only to snipers. Guy Chapman noted that the men of his company refused point blank to wear it after they had seen a sniper shot through the head the very first time he put one on. The French got theirs in 1915, though when the design had first been submitted in 1914, by Colonel Fenelon, Joffre had turned it down saying that the war would not last long enough to put it into mass production. The first 80,000 German *Stahlhelms* were issued to the troops at Verdun in January 1916, though more than a year elapsed before they became standard issue. The British helmet weighed almost 2 lbs, the French 18 ounces, and the German a ponderous $2\frac{1}{2}$ lbs.

Eventually, burdened as they were, the troops would stumble into their new position and the replaced unit would hurriedly assemble and make their own laborious way back down the communication trench. The company was then distributed between the fire trench and the support trench. Company headquarters were set up in a dugout and the men allocated their various duties. Like everything else the daily routine in a forward trench varied from unit to unit. Certain

French troops moving up to the front line.

features, however, were standard. The most important of these was that at all times some proportion of the men would be on sentry duty. The task was usually split into two or three-hour cycles. After a spell of sentry duty a man would take the same amount of sleep and then be available for a further two to three hours fatigues. At night the number of sentries was usually doubled, leaving even less time for sleep. Sheer exhaustion, in fact, was one of the greatest problems at the front. Sentries were often given beats to patrol, up and down the trench, and it was not uncommon to find a man who had fallen asleep on his feet and had wandered hundreds of yards away from his own unit. A private in the 5th Duke of Wellington's West Riding Regiment was of the opinion that 'the only thing that gets on one's nerves here is the sentry-go at night; we have really too much'. C.E. Montague wrote: 'For most of his time the average private was tired. Fairly often he was so tired as no man at home ever is in the common run of his work ... sometimes to the point of torment, sometimes much less, but always more or less tired.' In some units the sentries did not have a beat, but remained in one spot, peering through a steel loophole, a periscope, or simply staring over the parapet. Robert Graves explained:

> At night our sentries had orders to stand with their head and shoulders above the parapet...It implied greater vigilance and self-confidence in the sentry, and also put the top of his head above the level of the parapet. Enemy machine guns were trained on this level, and it would be safer to get hit in the chest or shoulders than in the forehead.

The whole twenty-four hour cycle in the trenches revolved round 'stand-to', just before dawn and dusk, when everybody mounted the fire step in case the enemy should choose this propitious moment to attack. The rest of the twenty-four hours was divided into two to four watches, those on duty being told to be particularly vigilant at night. After the dawn stand-to there would normally be a tacit truce for an hour or so, as each side prepared and ate its breakfast. In the Royal Fusilier trenches, in early 1915, breakfast was eaten at 8 a.m., after which rifles were inspected, fatigue parties were assembled to repair the trenches, and other work was done. Lunch was at noon, followed by more fatigues. Then dinner was taken at 6 p.m., followed by the dusk stand-to for about an hour, after which fatigue parties worked all night. In the 1st Cameronians in 1915 the dawn stand-to was at 4.10 a.m. At just after 5 a.m. one sentry per platoon would be mounted and the rest of the men would have their rifles inspected before either grabbing a little sleep or being assigned to a fatigue party. At dusk, after the stand-to, all men would fall in for an

officer's inspection. One third of them would then go on sentry duty, another third be dispatched down the communication trench for rations and stores from the Quartermaster, whilst the remaining third would sleep, work, or go out on patrols. In short, there was never any time, day or night, when the majority of the men were not awake and active. Accounts agree, however, that, as some sort of concession to normal pre-war habits, the quietest time of the whole twenty-four hours was between 3.30 a.m. and 9 a.m.

Particularly wearying were the endless fatigues. The trenches nearly always required some sort of repair or modification: they were not deep enough, the mud and water had to be cleared out, a sap dug, a new latrine sunk, or perhaps part of the line had subsided. Rations and stores had to be carried up from the trenches further back, or wounded men had to be carried back to the medical officer's dugout. And almost every night some men would have to crawl into no man's land to repair a gap in the wire or lay even more. Fatigues were just as endless in the support and reserve positions, where stores had to be continually moved around and complete new trench lines dug or existing ones remodelled. In the latter half of the war all sides began to realise that the soldiers simply could not sustain this dual role

of combat troops and porters *cum* navvies. The first British efforts in this direction were, at best, token gestures. In November 1915 Captain Hitchcock received an order from Divisional HQ decreeing that in future the word 'fatigue' was to be replaced by the word 'working party'. Somewhat later, both the British and the Germans began to form Labour Battalions to do the heavy trench·digging and road repairs, whilst the French used Territorial Regiments made up of older men not fit for active service. By the end of 1917, the Germans had 200 Labour Battalions and 100 Road Construction Battalions, all taken from *Landsturm* units, and the British had 300,000 men thus employed. Again they were men unfit for active service, the only qualification in the British Army being that a man was capable of marching three miles, doing three hours heavy labour, and marching three miles back. Those not up to it were assigned to clerical work in the rear areas.

The only men exempted from fatigues were those in the specialist units within the battalion or the division. Stretcher-bearers were usually exempt, as were bombers, the men trained to handle and throw grenades. Snipers, machine gunners and the 'Suicide Club' who fired the trench mortars were also usually spared the endless round of sentry duty and fatigues. In some units specific fatigues were assigned to particular men who were then exempted from other duties. In the London Rifle Brigade special wiring parties were formed,

who were excused normal trench hours, whilst in the 2nd Suffolks special groups of diggers were designated. The Germans seemed to have aimed at a system of incentives, for they laid it down that anyone promoted to the rank of *Gefreite*, Private 1st Class, should be excused all fatigues.

On the whole the daily round was no less gruelling for the officers. Whilst they rarely had to undertake heavy physical work, they too suffered from the chronic lack of sleep. As well as organising the fatigues and sentries, inspecting the men, visiting the sentries in the night and leading patrols, they had to cope with an inordinate amount of paperwork. They had to keep track of the trench stores, the mass of equipment that remained permanently in the trenches for the use of whatever unit was in the line at the time. These included planks, props, duckboards, coils of wire, bales of sandbags, small arms ammunition, grenades, picks, shovels, gas blankets, gas gongs, trench waders, Verey pistols, etc., and a detailed inventory had to be handed over to the relieving unit. On top of this casualty returns and daily occurrences in the line – working parties, trench improvements, enemy activity and the like. It seemed almost dangerous not to write down anything that happened: 'Now the motto ... is to write everything down, and in triplicate, if there is the least possible excuse for so doing. If you write enough, and do it according to form, you ought always to be able to shift the blame for anything that happens.'

Nor was the stream of paper a one-way traffic. Officers also had to digest a never-ending stream of memoranda and directives from higher commands. A German officer spoke of 'the stream of useless reports, questions and orders which pours in on us from above [which] can only be the result of disordered brains'. British front-line officers tended to refer to the daily Divisional situation report as 'Comic Cuts', and they too had their share of fatuous orders. During the first day of the Battle of the Somme a message reached the 1st Londons asking them to nominate a man to serve as a divisional drummer. In July 1916, an almost naked, exhausted soldier arrived in the trenches of an Australian unit, after running through an intensive artillery bombardment. His message was from the divisional vet and informed one of the officers; 'Sir, I have the honour to report that your old mare is suffering from an attack of the strangles.' A harassed French officer serving in the front-line Hartsmannswiller trenches one day received two urgent circulars. One informed him that buttons should always be sewn on with the embossed grenade the right way up. The other offered a final judgement of an equally weighty problem: a car flying a general's pennant should always be saluted, whether or not it was occupied.

The Things that Matter.

Scene: Loos, during the September offensive.
Colonel Fitz-Shrapnel receives the following message from "G.H.Q.":—
"Please let us know, as soon as possible, the number of tins of raspberry jam issued to you last Friday."

3 Natural Miseries

The world wasn't made in a day,
And Eve didn't ride in a bus,
But most of the world's in a sandbag,
And the rest of it's plastered on us.

Soldiers' doggerel

 And clink of shovels deepening the shallow trench.
The place was rotten with dead; green clumsy legs
High-booted, sprawled and grovelled along the saps
And trunks, face downward, in the sucking mud,
Wallowed like trodden sandbags loosely filled;
And naked sodden buttocks, mats of hair,
Bulged, clotted heads slept in the plastering slime.

Siegfried Sassoon

In the trenches men lived a life of primitive instincts – fear, hunger, thirst – and with the physical extremes, deafening noises, sudden flashes, extreme cold, agonising pain. Intellect and reason had almost no place. The most innocent of natural occurrences could be the cause of intense hardship. Rain is usually unpleasant; on the Western Front it became an implacable enemy. The battleground could not have been more unpropitious: Flanders has a particularly high rainfall and the land is almost at sea level, sometimes below it. Any attempt to dig down soon strikes water. Two of the British soldier's greatest enemies, in every season except summer, were water and mud. The trenches were invariably ankle-deep in mud, and often the level grew much higher. It was common for the water to be at least a foot deep and hardly rare for it to reach a man's thighs. There were actually occasions when men had to stand for days on end up to their waists, or even their armpits, in freezing water. Usually, of course, the water mixed with the earth in the trenches and turned to thick mud, making each step an effort. The shortest journey became a major enterprise. An officer of the 19th London Regiment, in the Ypres Salient in December 1916, told how it once took him three hours to make his way up a communication trench 400 yards long. The 1st Battalion of the Royal West Kent Regiment was posted to the same salient throughout the first winter of the war. It was not until April 1915, that they found even one communication trench that was passable without having to walk on the top of the trench.

A Canadian 'Scottie' helps a motor machine gun man out of difficulty.

The rain could come down at almost any time. Between 25 October 1914 and 10 March of the following year there were only eighteen dry days, and on eleven of these the temperature was below freezing. In March 1916, the rainfall was the heaviest for thirty-five years. In 1917, around Ypres and Passchendaele, at the height of the Third Battle of Ypres, it began drizzling on the 30 July and continued, without pause, for the whole of August. In July 1916, an officer of the London Regiment wrote home: 'The mud is awful. Have had two days of torrential rain which has flooded everything.' Throughout the war battalion reports were full of comments about the effects of the rain, particularly the mud. Sometimes men had to 'lie flat and distribute their weight evenly in order to prevent sinking in the mire'. One officer was ordered to consolidate his advanced position and wrote back 'It is impossible to consolidate porridge.' Mark Plowman wrote of the trenches on the Somme in November 1916:

> The mud makes it all but impassable, and now sunk in it up to the knees, I have the momentary terror of never being able to pull myself out. Such horror gives frenzied energy, and I tear my legs free and go on...Both sides are glued where they stand...Little or nothing is done for the simple reason that the deity has not yet constructed men able to make or repair trenches when the earth at every step holds them immobile.

In the same month one Guards battalion lost sixteen men through exhaustion and drowning in the mud. One had been trapped up to his neck in the stuff for forty-six hours, and though he was eventually rescued he died fifteen minutes later. On 12 December, Colonel Troyte-Bullock of the 7th Somerset Regiment, noted in his journal that 'the man who had sunk in up to his armpits had to be handed over as trench stores'.

The most horrible consequence of the mud was that men actually drowned in it. This sometimes happened in the trenches themselves, but more often when troops had been forced to climb out of an impassable communication trench and travel on top. The great danger then was of falling into a shell-hole and being slowly sucked down. A chaplain at the front told of a particularly horrible tale he was assured was true. A party of men from his division were going up to a sap head when, as they turned a corner in the trench, they stumbled across a man who had been blown into the mud. He was still alive, with only his head and the stump of a leg still visible. It proved impossible to get near enough to pull him out, and the party were forced to retrace their steps, leaving the wounded man to sink slowly. For the wounded, staggering back from an assault, even a shell-hole full of water could be a

death-trap. A survivor of the Third Battle of Ypres has desribed such an incident:

> A khaki-clad leg, three heads in a row, the rest of the bodies submerged, giving one the idea that they had used their last ounce of strength to keep their heads above the rising water. In another miniature pond, a hand still gripping a rifle is all that is visible, while its next-door neighbour is occupied by a steel helmet and half a head, the staring eyes staring icily at the green slime which floats on the surface almost at their level.

It was not only the British in Flanders who suffered from the effects of the weather. As one Frenchman wrote: 'Mud, the *poilus* had all sorts of names for it. But these names all boiled down to the same thing. Mud, be it known as *la melasse, la gadoue, la gadouille, la mouscaille.*' Each of these words, just as simple sounds, gives a vivid impression of the cloying, glutinous consistency of the mud. Another Frenchman noted that

> ... the communication trenches are no more than cess-pools filled with a mixture of water and urine. The trench is nothing more than a strip of water. The sides cave in behind you, as you pass, with a soft slither. We ourselves are transformed into statues of clay, with mud even in one's very mouth.

Another wrote in his diary:

> These days, a sea of mud. The badly wounded are drowned as they try to drag themselves to the aid post...The hardest trial is the mud...Dirty cartridges, rifles whose clogged up mechanisms won't work any more; the men pissed in them to make them fire.

In the slough of the Somme: rescuing a comrade from a shell hole. Wounded men often drowned in the mud.

Mules floundering through the mud, bringing up shells for the artillery.

A Canadian trooper takes off his great-coat for the last time.

There was little that could be done to alleviate the effects of the rain and the mud. The waterproof groundsheets served as some sort of protection, if used as a cape, and in late 1915 the British issued thigh-length gum-boots, to be used as trench stores; 2,500 pairs were allocated to each division. At about the same time, the Germans issued many pairs of waterproof overalls for the use of the men in the front-line trenches. The only other expedients were sumps, deep holes dug in the trench to drain off excess water, but these were only effective for very light rain and soon became clogged up. Miles and miles of duckboards were also laid along the floor of the trenches, but they often floated away or were trodden down into the mud. Also, because they were separate strips, laid end to end, walking along a pitch-black trench could be a hazardous excercise. If a man stepped on the very end of the board it tended to shoot up in the air and clout him on the nose or the back of the head.

Ironically, one of the men's most valuable protections, the great-coat, could prove a dreadful liability in wet weather. The coats weighed approximately 7 lbs. After a couple of days rain, however, they were capable of absorbing an extra 20 lbs of water. According to the Official History (Medical) it was quite common for the combination of mud and water to amount to an extra 34 lbs, and one officer reported that when the great-coats of a platoon coming out of the Somme trenches were weighed, one of them was actually 58 lbs. Added to over 60 lbs of equipment, it is clear that not the least of the ordeals of trench warfare was simply moving from one point to another. Imagine yourself in the pitch dark, after two or three days of wet, cold, hunger, sleeplessness, staggering down a trench, knee-deep in mud, carrying various burdens that almost equal your own body-weight.

The wet conditions were responsible for another abiding curse, 'trench foot', caused by having stood for hours, even days on end without being able to remove wet socks or boots. Just one immersion in water, followed by a twenty-four hour period during which the boots were never taken off was enough to cause trench foot. The condition was very similar to frost-bite, and was at first confused with it. The French, in fact, used the term *pieds gêlés* right through the war. The feet would gradually go numb, turn red or blue, and in extreme cases gangrene would set in. In this case, toes, or a whole foot, would have to be amputated.

Trench foot was recognised at an early stage in the war as a serious threat to a unit's effective strength. In 1914, there were only eight recorded cases; in 1915 the figure had reached 6,462. In March 1916, for example, after four days in the trenches at the Bluff, in Ypres, the 2nd Royal Scots had to exacuate 100 men, a quarter of their strength, who were suffering from exhaustion and trench foot. In the course of the

war 74,711 British troops were admitted to hospitals in France with trench foot or frost-bite. This was the second largest number of admissions for any particular condition, though only forty-one men actually died from it.

The only possible remedy was to try and ensure that the men changed their socks and dried their feet as often as possible. From late 1915 men carried up to three pairs of socks with them, which they were ordered to change once and more often twice a day. As well as vigorously drying their feet the men had also to coat them with a grease made of whale-oil before putting on the dry socks. On average a battalion used ten gallons of this noxious compound every day. From June 1917, the whale-oil began to be supplemented by a French mixture made of borated talcum powder and camphor.

But this system depended entirely on the front-line officers ensuring that the men did change their socks regularly. In the ceaseless round of activity it was easy to 'forget' or to succumb to the general apathy that prevailed in the appalling conditions. It is for this reason, presumably, that Robert Graves made a direct link between a unit's morale and the incidence of trench foot – though he overstates his case in saying that: 'Trench feet came only if [the soldier] did not mind getting trench feet, or anything else – because his battalion had lost the power of sticking things out.' What mattered was that a unit was sufficiently self-possessed to take the proper precautions. In another battalion that kept its cases of trench foot to the minimum each man of a company was responsible for the feet of another and had to ensure that he washed and powdered them at least once a day. If his charge got trench foot and went to hospital, he would find himself brought before the battalion commander. It was often impossible to find enough pairs of dry socks, either because they were simply not available in battalion stores or because they could not be dried out quickly enough. Some units developed a system whereby dry socks were brought up every night with the ration parties. Others found a more macabre solution. In 1917 a General Order had been posted that no man must return from the trenches without some piece of salvage – a tin helmet, a bomb, a Lewis drum, a barbed wire picket, etc. Guy Chapman's battalion was instructed to include socks amongst this list and the dead were always relieved of any pairs found in their haversacks. Getting the boots dry was even more difficult. Some units filled the boots with hot bran or with hot crumpled newspapers to try and

Artillery men posing for the camera in their fur coats. The rare white goat skin on the left was especially prized.

absorb the water. But no one ever found a really satisfactory solution simply because soldiers hardly ever had the chance to rest with their boots off for more than a couple of hours at a time, and that only occasionally.

Another related problem was cold. A lieutenant of the 2nd Scottish Rifles wrote:

> No one who was not there can fully appreciate the excruciating agonies and misery through which the men had to go in those days...Paddling about by day, sometimes with water above the knees; standing at night, hour after hour on sentry duty, while the drenched boots, puttees and breeches became stiff like cardboard with ice from the freezing cold air.

Life became a constant struggle to don enough clothes, and to stamp about and flail oneself with sufficient vigour to prevent the blood seemingly freezing in one's veins. The winter of 1916-17 was particularly savage. It lasted, implacably, from October to April, the severest since 1894-5. During January and February the conditions were positively Arctic. A sergeant of the 15th Australian battalion wrote:

> No water was brought [into the trenches], but the ice in the shell-holes was melted to obtain water...I filled my water-bottle at Mametz at midday with boiling hot tea, and when I reached Bull's Trench at 5 pm it was frozen so hard that an ordinary knife made hardly any impression on it, and we broke it instead.

Nor was the following winter much better. Again the first two months of the year were notably severe, with alternating periods of extreme cold and sudden thaw, the ideal recipe for mud and the sudden collapse of whole trenches. Rain, snow and sleet alternated from day to day. At an artillery observation post near Boesinghe the occupants began their tour standing up to their waists in water. By morning each of them was surrounded by a thin layer of ice.

There were only two possible antidotes to the cold. One was to provide heating in the dugouts and the other to make special clothing available. Most trenches, in fact, did have some sort of brazier in the dugout, using either coke or dry chips as fuel. But one had to pay a price even for keeping warm. The rank atmosphere in a fuggy dugout packed with dirty sweating men can well be imagined. There was rarely any chimney to extract the smoke and from time to time men died of asphyxiation whilst asleep. But if the braziers were kept outside the dugouts the problem then was to keep them alight. In November 1915, Hitchcock remembered seeing desperate German soldiers walking around on the parapets, swinging their braziers to and fro to keep the embers alive.

Some official provision was made for extra clothing. In late 1914, fur undercoats were issued, replaced a year later by sleeveless leather jerkins. The former were made of goatskin, the rare all-white ones being especially prized by those of a sartorial bent. Over this each man had his greatcoat and a mackintosh cape, the latter soon replaced by the combined waterproof cape/groundsheet. There was also an official issue of fingerless woollen gloves, whilst those who had to wear kilts in the trenches, a habit that was never abandoned, received a special issue of short woollen drawers. Beyond this the men had to make do with whatever cardigans, sweaters or mufflers they managed to get sent from home. The French were almost completely dependent on their own resourcefulness. Many stuffed newspapers in their jackets and down their trousers and wrapped thick bundles of rags around their feet. Several writers have commented on the bizarre appearance of French front-line troops in winter. C.M. Chenu described the terrible days of January 1915, when he saw 'an army of cowled phantoms, enveloped in blankets, strips of canvas, oil-cloth table covers'. Another wrote of men

> ...draped in canvas cloaks, like knights of old, wearing their helmet over their cap comforter and giving the appearance of some kind of ancient helm. Muffled up in strange woollens sent from home, their sheepskin capes made them look like the peasant soldiers of earlier days.

These various expedients were not without value. In the British Army, at least, the number of cases of pneumonia was, under the circumstances, remarkably low. The Medical History records only 7,827 cases, an average ratio of 1.52 per thousand men, although a high proportion of them, twelve per cent, proved fatal. What is even more extraordinary is that all sources agree that the common cold was almost unknown at the front. On the other hand, nephritis, which affects the kidneys and is generally attributable to excessive exposure to wet and cold, was a primary cause of non-battle casualies. 35,563 cases were admitted to hospitals in France, though only just over one per cent proved fatal.

Yet all the rain that fell on the Western Front was not enough to wash away the accumulated filth. The rubbish, urine, excreta, corpses in the trenches, as well as the unwashed state of the men, produced every type of pestilence and disease associated with such conditions. Sanitary facilities were crude at the best of times. Guy Chapman wrote of his spell at the front line on Tower Hamlets Ridge in 1917: 'We descended to primal man. No washing or shaving here, and the demands of nature answered as quickly as possible in the handiest and deepest shell-hole.' Officially, latrines in the trenches were to be pits four to five feet deep, placed in their

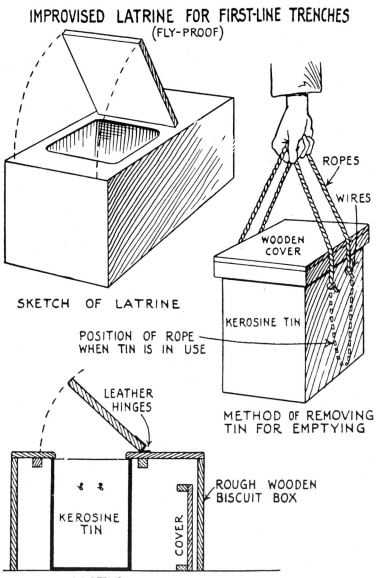

IMPROVISED LATRINE FOR FIRST-LINE TRENCHES
(FLY-PROOF)

SKETCH OF LATRINE

ROPES

WIRES

WOODEN COVER

KEROSINE TIN

POSITION OF ROPE WHEN TIN IS IN USE

METHOD OF REMOVING TIN FOR EMPTYING

LEATHER HINGES

KEROSINE TIN

COVER

ROUGH WOODEN BISCUIT BOX

SECTION

own sap. When filled within one foot of the top they were to be filled in and a new one dug. Sometimes provision was made for the use of metal buckets, again located in their own sap. When filled they were to be taken out somewhere between the front and support trenches and the contents dumped. Officially they were to be buried, but as often as not it was simply a case of hastily throwing the contents as far as possible. Or, as Chapman indicated, men would bypass the sanitary arrangements altogether and use a handy shell-hole. This must have at least earned the men the gratitude of the two sanitary personnel attached to each company. Usually referred to as the 'shit wallahs', one of their tasks was the disposal of urine and excreta.

Uncovering men who fell
contesting a crater at
Zouave Woods.

Corpses were an even greater hazard. Many men, particularly in the French lines, were buried almost where they fell. If a trench subsided, or new firebays or saps had to be dug, these bodies inevitably came to light. Similarly, when a new trench was dug, the working party would like as not come across large numbers of decomposing bodies buried just beneath the surface. These corpses, as well as the large amount of food scraps that littered the trenches, were an irresistible attraction to rats. These loathsome creatures are one of the commonest features of the descriptions of trench life. Both the Brown and the Black Rat were to be found, though the former were far more common, growing to astonishing proportions. A Canadian soldier recalled them many years later: 'Huge rats. So big they would eat a wounded man if he couldn't defend himself.' Worse, they were very fecund. If well fed they produce more and bigger litters, and in ideal conditions *one* couple might produce some 880 offspring in a year. They were also extremely bold. To get at food they would swarm around a dugout whether or not it was occupied. They would scamper over the faces of sleeping men, sometimes burrowing under their blankets or snuffling for food in their pockets. Even when men hung their food from the roof they would wake to find a sleek, filthy acrobat gnawing at its prize. But their greatest favourite was a corpse. Particularly succulent were the eyes and livers. Barbusse notes that one would always find two or three dead rats around a corpse, where they had either surfeited or poisoned themselves. Usually one would also find as many live rats, often having burrowed their way right into the corpse. A French soldier tells a typical story:

> One evening, whilst on patrol, Jacques saw some rats running from under the dead men's greatcoats, enormous rats, fat with human flesh. His heart pounding, he edged towards one of the bodies. Its helmet had rolled off. The man displayed a grimacing face, stripped of flesh; the skull bare, the eyes devoured. A set of false teeth slid down on to his rotting jacket, and from the yawning mouth leapt an unspeakably foul beast.

Efforts to get rid of the rats were sporadic and half-hearted. They lived on in their tens of millions, provoking revulsion, contaminating food and spreading disease. Though they never precipitated any plague-like outbreak, the rats were known to be the carriers of at least one serious disease. This was an infective jaundice known as Weil's Disease which became widespread during the last two years of the war.

The other great scourge of the trenches was lice, an

inevitable and constant companion of every man in the trenches. Eric Partridge remembered the lice, or chatts as they were usually known, vividly:

> They were a pale fawn in colour, and left blotchy red bite marks all over the body except in the hair of the head. They also created a distinctive sour, stale smell...On the other hand, captured German dugouts on the Western Front sometimes had a species of small red lice crawling over their walls and blankets. [A Frenchman wrote:] 'The lice feared solitude and had a profound sense of family...Lice have a very warm, very soft bedroom, where the table is always laid. There, in their numerous moments of leisure, they followed the counsels of the creator: they multiplied'.

Various methods were used to minimise their attentions. In spare moments men would launch major offensives on their shirts and underclothes, either running their fingernails up the seam or running a candle along it. The latter skill was only learnt with practice and many a garment was scorched or burnt right through. The unfortunate Scots suffered particularly as their kilts, with their numerous pleats, offered a refuge for hundreds of lice. The individual methods of the men were supplemented by more organised methods. The first, instituted in 1915, was the Divisional Baths, usually in an old brewery where, if they were lucky, the men would go about once a week. There, after soaping themselves in some

Australian trooper receives his issue of new underwear after delousing.

sort of foot bath, the men would plunge into huge vats of hot water, ten or twelve men at a time, and splash around for fifteen minutes or so as their tunics and trousers were put through the 'Foden Disinfector' or delousing machine. They were then brushed and ironed and given back to the men, along with clean shirts and underwear. The soiled underwear was piled in lorries and sent back to the Corps Laundry. Unfortunately the delousing process was of little use. A fair proportion of the eggs remained in the clothes and within two or three hours of their being put on again a man's body heat had hatched them out. One then had to suffer and scratch for at least another week.

At one stage some theorist suggested to the War Office that they might try impregnating the troops' underwear with a chemical so noxious that it would kill any louse that came into contact with it. A party of kilted volunteers was put into quarantine to test this idea. At night the men were deliberately infected with lice and in the day they wore the special drawers and vests sent by the War Office. The results were a ludicrous failure. As the officer in charge wrote of the day-time marches that the men were sent on:

> After a mile or two some of the men began to complain of an itching of the skin...Often I had to permit the more frenzied to remove their underclothes and march carrying these in their hands...Apart from their marches they lived a carefree life...They all put on weight, their physiques and appetites improved; the same applied, unfortunately, to the lice.

Not only did the lice cause frenzied scratching, they also carried disease, and one which proved to be a continual and heavy drain on manpower. This was known as trench fever or, with disarming honesty, 'pyrrexhia of unknown origin'. The two conditions were diagnosed separately but were almost certainly the same disease. The Germans showed a similar lack of precision, calling it variously Wolhynian Fever, Five Days Fever, Polish, Russian, Intermittent, or Meuse Fever. First noticed in 1915, the actual connection with the louse was not made until early 1918, and no cure was found until the end of the war. A common preliminary symptom were acute shooting pains in the shins, after which a high fever would set in. It was never fatal, but treatment necessitated between six weeks and three months off duty. In 1917 it accounted for fifteen per cent of all cases of sickness in the British Army.

Rats and lice were by far the most ubiquitous and unpleasant of the natural miseries at the front. But there were others. In summer especially, flies swarmed about the dugouts in their thousands, settling on any exposed food. Nor were they averse to the human body. A British officer, with a typical nonchalant precision, noted after waking up in a dugout on the Somme that there were seventy-two flies on his pyjama arm between the wrist and the shoulder. On getting out of bed he counted a further thirty-two dead ones in his shaving water, which his servant had only just brought in. French descriptions are more graphic. J. Germain, with the 55th Division in Artois, in July 1915, wrote: 'An immense cloud smelling of corpses swept the plateau incessantly, choking the combatants with its fetid odour. Thousands of flies with blue and green stomachs covered the countryside, shrouded our meagre rations...and hid the sky in a shimmering cloud.' Another described a more ghastly aspect. One morning, 'on our shoulders fell a rain of maggots, which all through the night, above our heads, had made a noise like rustling silk as they gnawed their way through some dead man's guts'.

Nits infested the men's hair, which is why every company soon had its own barber to shave them to the very skull. Many objected to this and tried to at least keep a reasonable amount of hair on top of their heads, where it would be hidden by their caps. It was for this reason that when the men were being paid, as each man stepped forward to receive his money, he had to take his cap off. Any man whose hair was not short enough had the money credited to him, until he had visited the barber. But Army bureaucracy was so ponderous that he would be lucky if he ever saw it again that side of the Armistice. There were also itch mites which caused scabies as the men scratched their skins and infected it. A French Casualty Clearing Station drew up some figures about its work in 1917. Out of a total of 106,167 admissions (battle and non-battle casualties) 26,879 were cases of scabies, boils and other skin diseases. Another 26,024 cases were types of trench fever, myalgia or rheumatism. In other words, almost fifty per cent of the casualties were directly attributable to the appalling conditions in the trenches. The British figure for the whole war present a similar picture. On the Western Front, between 1914 and 1918, 2,690,054 men became battle casualties and 3,528,486 succumbed to sickness and disease. Serving on the Western Front was not simply a problem of avoiding being blown up or shot. However the sick had a far better chance of surviving than the wounded. Thirty-one per cent of battle casualties eventually died as against less than one per cent of the sick.

A final natural misery of trench warfare was the stench. This is alluded to in almost every contemporary account, yet it is almost impossible to convey accurately. It was compounded of a score of things: the chloride of lime that was liberally scattered to minimise the risk of infection, the creosol that was sprayed around to get rid of the flies, the contents of the latrines, the smoke from the braziers and the sweat of the men.

Henri Barbusse reembered being continually woken up by the
sickening odour of men's feet as they marched down the
trench, past his head. But predominantly it was a smell of
putrefaction. One British private said that his 'overriding
memory of all his time on the Western Front was the smell'.
Another in his diary, spoke of 'a penetrating and filthy
stench…a combination of mildew, rotting vegetation and the
stink which rises from the decomposing bodies of men and
animals. This smell seems a permanent feature of the firing
line.' The odour was almost unbearable in the great charnel
houses of the front, Ypres, the Somme, Verdun. When the
Germans captured Côte 304 at Verdun in May 1916 one of the
first demands of the conquering troops was for a double ration
of tobacco to mask the overwhelming stink of the corpses. A
Frenchman who fought in this sector wrote 'We all had on us
the stench of dead bodies. The bread we ate, the stagnant
water we drank, everything we touched had a rotten smell,
owing to the fact that the earth around us was literally stuffed
with corpses.'

Flies feeding on dead Germans.

4 Guns and Gas

After crawling out through the bleeding remnants of my comrades, and through the smoke and debris, wandering and running in the midst of the raging gunfire in search of refuge, I am now awaiting death at any moment. You do not know what Flanders means. Flanders means endless human endurance. Flanders means blood and scraps of human bodies. Flanders means heroic courage and faithfulness even unto death.

Letter found on the body of an unknown German officer.

Though the soldiers hardly ever saw their adversary, they were continually made aware of his presence, even in the 'quietest' of sectors. Any unit in the trenches would always sustain casualties, whether ordered to go over the top or simply to stay put. Charles Carrington relates that in one spell of three front-line tours, eighteen days in all, the battalion lost one third of its strength. Fifty of these were battle casualties and the rest were men taken sick. During two months in the Neuve Chapelle sector, in late 1916, the 13th Yorkshire and Lancashire lost 255 men though they had been on the defensive throughout the whole period. General Headquarters made an estimate of the expected wastage of men over a typical twelve-month period. In six months of a large-scale offensive they reckoned on losing 513,252 men and in six months of 'ordinary' trench warfare, 300,000. The most common cause of battle casualties when in the trenches was enemy artillery fire. On almost every day at least some shells would fall on the trenches, killing, maiming or burying a few unfortunates. Nor were villages behind the line immune, receiving their daily quota of heavier shells as in Ploegsteert Wood in 1915 where five or six shells landed in the village each day. Worse, no troops were entirely safe from their own artillery. A French general has estimated, though it is difficult to imagine on what evidence, that some 75,000 Frenchmen

became victims of their own guns. Sidney Rogerson of the 2nd Battalion the West Yorkshire Regiment, recalled that 'the PBI had suffered heavily during recent weeks from their own artillery, which was why we were prepared to damn the gunners without reflecting upon the difficulty of their task'. The Germans, too, had their problems in this respect. One

'The tense moment when an order arrives by field telephone from the observation officer.'

particularly incompetent unit, the 49th Field Artillery Regiment, was known as the 48½th because its shells persistently fell short.

In quantative terms alone the artillery war staggers the imagination. During the war the British fired off over 170 million rounds of all types – more than five million tons. The expenditure on ammunition was particularly awesome. In one day in September 1917 almost a million rounds were fired. During the first two weeks of the Third Battle of Ypres 4,283,550 rounds were fired at a cost of £22,211,389 14s. 4d.

Barrages were not always so intensive. In a light barrage, usually in the afternoon, one could expect about half a dozen shells to land in the immediate vicinity every ten minutes. In a big bombardment, often the prelude to an enemy assault, howitzers supplemented the ordinary field guns, and twenty

to thirty shells would be landing in a company sector every minute. For every three to four heavy explosive howitzer shells there would be one shrapnel to make sure the troops kept their heads down. Suddenly the barrage would lift and then, five minutes later, start up again. As the evening wore on the intervals would get shorter and shorter and the almost continuous noise grow to a crescendo.

To experience this type of bombardment was a physical and mental torture. Writers have used all kinds of similes and metaphors to convey their experiences. If in a deep dugout a bombardment was just about bearable, Captain Greenwell found that 'the main impression gathered from the depths of a dugout is of a series of noises never heard before, though faintly resembling what I should imagine a tropical thunderstorm at sea to be like'. Later on he qualifies this rather romantic image 'Modern warfare...reduces men to shivering beasts. There isn't a man who can stand shell-fire of the modern kind without getting the blues.' The noise could be fearsome. 'It was as if on some overhead platform ten thousand carters were tipping loads of pointed steel bricks that burst in the air or on the ground, all with a fiendish, devastating ear-splitting roar that shook the nerves of the stoutest.' Lieutenant Chandos of the 2nd Grenadier Guards wrote: 'If you want the effect of an 8.5 bursting near you, stand at the edge of the platform when an express is coming through at sixty miles per hour, and imagine that it runs into a siding about twenty yards away.' Yet, as the same officer wrote 'The sensation of this sort of artillery fire is not that of sound. You feel it in your ears more than hear it, unless it is only about one hundred yards away.' Many other soldiers took up this theme of the barrage being more than mere sound, of a noise that was so continuous and so deafening that it was almost tangible. Henri Barbusse wrote:

A diabolical uproar surrounds us. We are conscious of a sustained crescendo, an incessant multiplication of the universal frenzy; a hurricane of hoarse and hollow banging of raging clamour, of piercing and beast-like screams, fastens furiously with tatters of smoke upon the earth where we are buried up to our necks, and the wind of the shells seems to set it heaving and pitching.

An NCO of the 22nd Manchester Rifles described the bombardment on the first day of the Battle of the Somme:

The sound was different, not only in magnitude but in quality, from anything known to me. It was not a succession of explosions or a continuous roar; I, at least, never heard either a gun or a bursting shell. It was not a noise, it was a symphony. And it did not move. It hung over us. It seemed as though the air were full of vast and agonised passion, bursting now with groans and sighs, now into shrill screaming and pitiful whimpering, shuddering beneath terrible blows, torn by unearthly whips, vibrating with the solemn pulses of enormous wings. And the supernatural tumult did not pass in this direction or in that. It did not begin, intensify, decline and end. It was poised in the air, a stationary panorama of sound, a condition of the atmosphere, not the creation of man.

A Lewis gun emplacement after a German bombardment.

A Canadian private recalled similar sensations during the barrage that preceded the assault on Vimy Ridge: 'One's whole body seemed to be in a mad macabre dance...I felt that if I lifted a finger I should touch a solid ceiling of sound, it now had the attribute of solidity.'

But much worse than the purely physical effect of the noise was the effect on the nerves, the feeling of powerlessness, a total and utterly enervating feeling of vulnerability. A Frenchman at Verdun wrote that the battle was so 'terrible...because man is fighting against material, with the sensation of striking out at empty air'. A German private cursed 'the torture of having to lie powerless and defenceless in the middle of an artillery battle'. It became difficult to hang on to one's sanity. Lance-Corporal Hearn of the Durham Light Infantry dreaded the 'horrible nightmare of bursting shells. Sometimes the terrible noise makes me nearly mad, and it requires a great effort to keep cool, calm and collected'. A French infantry sergeant gave a description of the mental anguish:

When one heard the whistle in the distance, one's whole body continued to resist the too excessively potent vibrations of the explosion, and at each repetition it was a new attack, a new fatigue, a new suffering. Under this regime, the most solid nerves cannot resist for long; the moment arrives where the blood rises to the head, where fever burns the body and where the nerves, exhausted, become incapable of reacting. It is as if one were tied tight to a post and threatened by a fellow swinging a sledgehammer. Now the hammer is swung back for the blow, now it whirls forward, till, just missing your skull, it sends the splinters flying from the post once more. This is exactly what it feels like to be exposed to heavy shelling.'

Men gradually lost control of themselves as the strain mounted. They began to moan to themselves and whimper like helpless animals. An English doctor wrote: 'I remember...a private in one of the four crack French corps who was at Douaumont in the Verdun battle told his parents that by the ninth day [of the barrage] almost every soldier was crying.' In some cases, at the end of a heavy bombardment, when the enemy finally began to push forward, they would find their opponents apparently asleep in the trenches, comatose, utterly and totally exhausted by the strain. Even for those who remained partially alert, the end of a bombardment, or a temporary lull, did not lessen the sense of horror. A variety of sounds might be heard in the sudden quiet; the ghostly wail of a shell's screw-cap as it whizzed through the air after an explosion, the plaintive moaning of the men, the buzzing of great swarms of flies, disturbed by the bombardment, the high-pitched screaming of the rats, and, sublime absurdity, the singing of the birds.

Gas

One particularly horrible type of shell were those that released gas. It was also discharged from cylinders, though this made the wind direction a particularly crucial consideration. Gas was first used at the Second Battle of Ypres on 22 April 1915, and the victims were a regiment of French colonial troops, who panicked completely, throwing down their rifles and fleeing to the rear. After this both sides began to use gas and experimented with different types. At first chlorine gas was the most common but this was later superseded by mustard gas, the cause of the most casualties. In the American Army out of nearly 58,000 gas casualties, 26,828 were known to have

been due to mustard gas. Its smell belied its effect. One 'doughboy' likened it to a rich bon-bon filled with perfumed soap. Chlorine gas, on the other hand, was rather like a mixture of pineapple and pepper, whereas phosgene had more the stench of a barrel of rotten fish. But each had its own ghastly effects. The chlorine gases led to a slow death by asphyxiation, and even the hopeless cases often took days to die, remaining conscious to within five minutes of the end. 'There, sitting on the bed, fighting for breath, his lips plum-coloured, his hue leaden, was a magnificent young Canadian past all hope in the asphyxia of chlorine...I shall never forget the look in his eyes as he turned to me and gasped: "I can't die! Is it possible that nothing can be done for me?"' Wilfred Owen of the Manchester Regiment, the poet, wrote of a man exposed to phosgene gas:

> ...the white eyes writhing in his face,
> His hanging face, like a devil's sick of sin;
> If you could hear, at every holt, the blood
> Come gargling from the froth-corrupted lungs,
> Obscene as cancer, bitter as the cud
> Of vile, incurable sores on innocent tongues...

With mustard gas the effects did not become apparent for up to twelve hours. But then it began to rot the body, within and without. The skin blistered, the eyes became extremely painful and nausea and vomiting began. Worse, the gas attacked the bronchial tubes, stripping off the mucous membrane. The pain was almost beyond endurance and most cases had to be strapped to their beds. Death took up to four or five weeks. A nurse wrote:

I wish those people who write so glibly about this being a holy war and the orators who talk so much about going on no matter how the long the war lasts and what it may mean, could see a case – to say nothing of ten cases – of mustard gas in its early stages – could see the poor things burnt and blistered all over with great mustard-coloured suppurating blisters, with blind eyes...all sticky and stuck together, and always fighting for breath, with voices a mere whisper, saying that their throats are closing and they know they will choke.

Some sort of precaution was available almost immediately after the first gas attack. One division sent a sanitary officer hot-foot to Paris to commandeer all the ladies' veiling he could find. The first anti-gas drill consisted of men running round in circles, holding noses and grasping between their teeth pledgets of tow soaked in hyposulphite and wrapped in ladies' veils. Within sixty hours 98,000 pads of cotton waste in muslin containers were available at the front, two million having been provided at the end of the first month. Another early expedient was to clasp pads soaked in urine to one's nose and mouth. Unpleasant an experience as this was the ammonia in the urine did help to neutralise the chlorine. Later in the year a larger block gauze pad was used. Tied with

Men blinded by tear gas at an advanced dressing station.

67

tapes it had an extra flap to cover the eyes. Troops were provided with a bottle of hyposulphite solution in which to soak the pad. The next expedient was a grey flannel hood with mica eye-pieces, impregnated with phenol. After this there followed two types of tube-helmet, so called, which were the same as the hood with the addition of a rubber-tipped metal tube, to be held between the teeth for exhalation, and better fitting eye-pieces. From late 1917, the famous box respirator replaced all these devices and was soon standard issue for troops at the front. All in all, some twenty-seven million gas-masks of various types were manufactured in Britain during the war.

Snipers

In one fortnight of trench warfare in December 1915, British troops sustained a total of 3,285 wounds. About twenty-three per cent of these were in the head, face and neck. It is a fair assumption that a great number of this latter category were caused by snipers. Though these marksmen were not as terrifying as the big bombardments or as burdensome as the mud, they did present a constant irritation, picking off anyone who showed his head even for a split-second. In early 1915 one officer wrote: 'Sergeant Doherty was killed by a sniper whilst supervising a building fatigue. This is the eighteenth casualty and the fourth NCO we have lost in this way since we came into the line on Tuesday – it is a frustrating business.' In the Vermelles sector in September 1916, an officer of the West Yorkshires who popped his head above the parapet for a quick look was hit twice by two different snipers.

Walter Schmidt, the crack German sharp shooter, 1917. Note the telescopic sight.

As with most of the innovations of trench warfare, the Germans were the first to use snipers in a methodical way. Particularly adept shots were ear-marked as marksmen and given a special oak-leaf badge. They wore camouflaged capes, carried their own steel loop-holes. and usually had rifles with telescopic sights. Throughout the war the Germans had many more of these latter than their opponents. British snipers had to draw their rifles with Ross telescopic sights from the very limited stock held by the battalion sniping officer. The German snipers worked in units and these remained in the same sector for months on end, free unlike their British counterparts, from the normal rotation of trench garrisons. In this way they acquired an intimate knowledge of the terrain, knowing every good vantage point, every exposed junction, and every gap in the parapet. Until 1917, the British left the organisation of snipers to the individual units. In the 7th Battalion of the Royal West Kents for example, gamekeepers were employed to form a twenty-four man detatchment, specifically for sniping. In July 1917 however, orders were given that each company should supply two of its best shots to join a sniper section attached to brigade or division

A dummy tree on Hill 63, used by Australian snipers during the battle of Messines, June 1917.

headquarters. These men were to work in pairs, one selecting targets and computing ranges, the other actually loosing off the bullet.

The snipers' methods were much the same on both sides. The fixed steel loop-hole was unpopular because the enemy marksmen very soon got a bead on it. One either carried the loop-hole around or avoided it altogether. In some areas, because of the excellence of the opposing snipers, marksmen preferred to bob up over the parapet and fire a couple of snapshots at a spot they had already picked out. The most important consideration, in all cases, was to keep on the move. It was a rule never to fire off more than two or three or shots from the same spot, and never to return to a spot once one had moved on. Usually the snipers did not operate in the trenches themselves, but crept out at dawn into no man's land, and remained there all day, moving from cover to cover. Most of them wore camouflaged clothing and sometimes even more elaborate measures were adopted. Hollow trees had their advocates, and beneath Pilkem Ridge the British went so far as to construct a mock steel-lined tree trunk. A common German ruse was to send up a kite or brandish a sign with English lettering on it. Anyone foolish enough to raise his head to try and read it was immediately shot. Such ploys were a common feature of counter-sniper work. When a German marksman became particularly troublesome, the British often brought their artillery to bear. Attempts would be made to draw his fire by raising a dummy torso above the parapet, exposing a cap or helmet, or even risking a quick look. If the sniper fired, a compass bearing would be taken on the direction, and if the artillery observation post could then locate the exact spot, a short barrage would be delivered on to the position. In this new warfare of material might, individual finesse provoked only massive retaliation.

PART TWO

Over the Top

5 Patrols and Raids

We had no light to see by, save the flares.
On such a trail, so lit, for ninety yards
We crawled on belly and elbows, till we saw,
Instead of lumpish dead before our eyes,
The stakes and crosslines of the German wire.
We lay in shelter of the last dead man,
Ourselves as dead, and heard their shovels ring
Turning the earth, then talk and cough at times.
A sentry fired and a machine gun spat;
They shot a flare above us, when it fell
And spluttered out in the pools of No Man's Land,
We turned and crawled past the remembered dead:
Past him and him, and them and him...
And through the wire and home, and got our rum.

A.G. West

The ordinary soldier was only occasionally involved in a full-scale attack. Going over the top usually meant a patrol into no man's land to secure information about the enemy's dispositions and level of preparedness. They were usually very small, made up of an officer and one or two men. German patrols tended to be bigger – often six or seven men though generally no officer was present. For a period in 1916 every battalion in the British Army had a special scouting platoon. But this plan was soon abandoned and all men and junior regimental officers had to take it in turns to go out on patrol. It was felt that this nerve-wracking activity somehow kept up the 'offensive spirit'. The patrols always went out at night. They would cautiously inch their way forward on their stomachs and try to get within earshot of the enemy trenches. There one might hear the snatch of a conversation or the sound of some untoward activity. Occasionally some forward sentry or the member of an enemy patrol might be captured.

In fact, men's nerves became so taut that they found it very difficult to be sure exactly what they had seen or heard, if anything. Alan Thomas of the 6th Royal West Kents seems to have remembered the experience with some pleasure:

Scrambling over the parapet always gave one a kick. Taking your bearings you made for the gap in [your own] wire...Once through...the fun – if you can call it that – began. Every object seemed to take on human shape. If you gazed at it long enough you could swear that it was moving...Nearing the German lines one might (or might not) catch some sound of the enemy – a voice, a footfall, the metallic sound of a rifle being shifted, or maybe only a

Gas alarm at Loos. Note the shell casing (on the left) being used as a warning bell.

'What it really feels like to be on patrol duty at night time'. A Bruce Bairnsfather cartoon.

cough or the clearing of a throat…Even then you might find that what you had been listening to was nothing but the sound of loose wire blowing in the wind.

A French sergeant, with the 161st Infantry in the Argonne, described a similar problem:

We slid forward imperceptibly, moving on our elbows and knees, our left hands gripping the handle of our bayonets. I scoured the Bosch trenches with an intense gaze, but not fixedly, for if you keep on staring into the pitch blackness, vague shadows seem to appear, immobile objects seem to move and imagination takes over from precise observation.

In fact, however, the purpose of the patrol was as much morale as to gather information. Great store was laid at divisional level, and higher, on the importance of gaining the 'upper hand' in no man's land and not letting the enemy feel that he could crawl about with impunity. At the front line itself most men were not too bothered about such questions. For them the essential point was to remain alive. When opposing patols stumbled across each other, as sometimes happened, a spirit of live and let live often prevailed. A private of the 4th King's Royal Rifle Corps has told how in one part of the front a road ran through no man's land. When a patrol reached that road it would place a helmet on an upturned rifle. When the opposing patrol reached the same spot it too would erect an identical sign. Both sides would then sit tight for an hour or so, without actually meeting, and then quietly return to their own trenches. Similar etiquette applied when wiring parties ran into one another. Private Gilbert Hall of the 13th Yorkshire and Lancashire remembered how both parties would carry on working and tacitly ignore each other. But as soon as one side was back in the trenches, firing would break out. The wiring thus became a frantic race to see who could finish work first. In many sectors where the trenches were close together it was a standard quip that the opposing wiring parties were sharing the same mallets.

For all this going out on patrol was an extremely nerve-wracking enterprise. As one cowered in a shell-hole, or slowly crawled a little further forward every tiny sound or movement – a scuttling rat, one's equipment creaking, a sentry moving, a flare suddenly bursting above, made one feel utterly exposed. The effort of not making a noise was a particular strain. A lieutenant of Princess Patricia's Canadian Light Infantry thought that almost the

…hardest thing on your nerves was litter in no man's land. The tin cans, the sheets of corrugated iron, the hundreds of seemingly loose pieces of barbed wire which always turned out to be solidly anchored at the other end and so sent you sprawling among all that lethal and noisy junk.

And there were worse things than junk. No man's land was littered with bodies. Arthur Graeme West of the Public Schools Battalion described them in his poem *The Night Patrol*:

British troops cut their way through wire while on a night patrol.

> ...and everywhere the dead.
> Only the dead were always present – present
> As a vile sickly smell of rottenness;
> The rustling stubble and the early grass,
> The slimy pools – the dead men stank throughall,
> Pungent and sharp; as bodies loomed before,
> And as we passed they stank: then dulled away
> To that vague foetor, all encompassing,
> Infecting earth and air.

Those who got back safely from patrols felt drained and exhausted. A French soldier has described the peculiar introversion that afflicted men as they crawled back into their trenches:

> You...feel like an outlaw, exiled and untouchable. You are, in any case, utterly exhausted. The prostration is a nervous reaction and that is why, no matter what their military effectiveness, I compare missions like this to the effect of drugs on the human consciousness. A patrol is a massive dose...You go out and come back – that is if you come back at all – a changed man.

The High Command had another technique for maintaining the illusion of an offensive posture. This was the trench raid, a much bigger enterprise than the patrol and with the avowed intent of actually entering the enemy lines. They seem to have been started by the British, but there is some dispute as to who actually conducted the first one. Some say the Canadians, whilst another source gives the credit to the First and Second Battalions of the Gerwhal Rifles, an Indian unit on 9/10 November 1914. Whatever the truth, raids soon became a widely accepted device. Their aim was two-fold, to prevent the front-line troops from adopting a completely passive attitude and to gather information about the enemy by bringing back prisoners, insignia from bodies or documents.

A typical raiding party would comprise about thirty men, often volunteers, from one company. The men would be thoroughly briefed about the purposes of the raid and the topography of the enemy trenches. In many cases they would spend three or four days behind the lines practising the raid on dummy entrenchments. Provision would be made for an artillery bombardment before and during the raid. Before the raid the enemy trenches themselves would be hit; during it, a 'box barrage' would be laid down around the target area to prevent enemy reinforcements being sent up. From about 1916 the Germans became particularly adept at this, referring to such a mission as a 'winkle raid'.

German barrage fire at night.

Just before the raid began the men prepared themselves. They had to divest themselves of all equipment that might either hinder movement or reveal the identity of their unit. Collar flashes and regimental buttons were taken off, the latter being replaced by toggles or safety pins. Pay-books and all personal letters were left behind, though the raiders were allowed to carry a small slip of paper giving their Army number, so that the Germans could notify the Red Cross of their fate if the need arose. Steel helmets were removed and replaced with woollen cap-comforters. All water-bottles and haversacks were left behind, and only a skeleton webbing was worn with ammunition pouches attached. Some units even attached rubber bars to the men's boots, and it was standard procedure for everyone to blacken their faces with grease-paint or burnt cork. At first raiders carried the standard rifle and bayonet, but as the war went on more specialised weapons were evolved. Rifles were specially cut down. A fearsome array of truncheons, coshes and knobkerries were designed by the men themselves, and any sort of sheath-knife was also popular.

One of the most popular weapons of all, particularly with the higher commands, was the grenade. Once again one sees how the peculiar conditions of the Western Front forced men to delve back into history and rediscover weapons and techniques that had been developed hundreds of years before. In the European armies of 1914 the word 'grenadier' was merely an honorary appellation, harking back to specialised

Mills bombers blast German machine-gunners out of their positions.

companies of the seventeenth and early eighteenth centuries. Yet within a year or so most troops were again familiar with these antique devices. Queen Anne's grenadiers might well have looked aghast at some of the crude bombs the men were expected to throw about.

Before the advent of the familiar pineapple-like Mills Bomb in the spring of 1915, British hand grenades were of many types, though most of them were as dangerous to their users as to the enemy. One early model was known as the Newton Pippin and its fuse was ignited by rapping it against the handle of the entrenching tool. Another was fired like some enormous match by striking it against the side of a match-box. In 1915 the so-called 'jam-pot' bomb became popular. The Official History accurately conveys the amateurishness of these devices:

> Take a jam-pot [in fact a tin], fill it with shredded gin cotton and ten penny nails, mixed according to taste. Insert a No.8 detonator and a short length of Bickford's Fuse. Clamp up the lid. Light with a match, pipe, cigar or cigarette and throw for all you are worth.

German infantryman hurls his 'Potato Masher' grenade at the British lines.

Other grenades to be found in the early months of the war were the 'Battye' bomb, a four by two inch cast-iron cylinder filled with ammonal and sealed with a wooden plug, and the 'Hairbrush', a slab of gun cotton taped on to a hairbrush-shaped piece of wood. Both were ignited in the same bonfire-night manner as the 'jam-pot'. The Germans had two basic types of grenade. The 'Tortoiseshell', a flat circle with strikers all round the circumference to detonate on impact, and the famous 'Potato Masher', a nine-inch cylinder on the end of a five-inch wooden handle, with streamers at the end to make it more steady in flight.

These grenades were the basic weapon of a raiding party. Once in the trench, the raiders tried to bomb their way from traverse to traverse. The men went along the trench in single file, with two men with bayonet fixed in front, two bombers, an officer, and a tail of 'understudies' and bomb carriers. At each new traverse the bombers would let fly, and then the bayonet men would rush round the traverse to finish off any survivors. The Germans were equally keen on the grenade as a defensive weapon in such encounters and rarely had recourse to rifles or bayonets. Charles Carrington says that he never actually saw a German soldier with his bayonet fixed throughout the war. General Harper, who rose to be commander of the 4th Corps, once asserted that 'No man in this war has ever been killed with the bayonet unless he had his hands up first'. British casualty figures show that out of one sample of over 200,000 wounds, only 0.32 per cent of them were caused by bayonets. The American Surgeon General's report, for the whole war, gives only 0.024 per cent. It is possible, however, to make a little too much of this redundancy of 'cold steel' in the new type of warfare. It should not be forgotten that the vast percentage of bayonet wounds were immediately fatal, and thus never entered the casualty returns. Also this weapon was so menacing that often one did not actually have to use it; immediate surrender or flight were the most common reactions. The British High Command were certainly convinced of its potential. They employed a special officer, Colonel Campbell, to tour the front giving bloodthirsty lectures on the techniques of bayonet fighting.

But no matter what the techniques trench raiding was never a popular activity:

How these raids came to be abominated by those who had to make them! To judge from what appeared in some of the newspapers, as well as the official communiqués...the British soldier longed, above all things, to be allowed to take part in a raid. If this was indeed the case he certainly concealed this desire very successfully from his friends.

Many felt that raids had no particular strategic value, but were merely the product of staff jealousies, a search for prestige bought with other men's blood. Writing in his diary in January 1917 an officer noted: 'After a time these raids became unpopular with regimental officers and the rank and file, for there grew up a feeling that sometimes these expeditions to the enemy trenches owed their origin to rivalry between organisations higher than battalions.'

Germans captured at Pilkem. Note the fortified blockhouse at the rear.

6 Battle: Strategy and Tactics

Why are they dead? Is Adam's seed so strong
That these bold lives cut down mean nothing lost?
Indeed, they would have died: ourselves ere long
Will take their turn. That cheque is signed and crossed.
But, though this dying business still concerns
The lot of us, there seems something amiss
When twenty million funeral urns
Are called for. Have you no hypothesis?

Edmund Blunden

Clearly, not even the High Commands ever believed that trench raids alone would do much to end the war. All sides agreed that the basic aim must be to break the deadlock of trench warfare. Some way had to be found to rupture the enemy lines and restore the balance between offence and defence. From the very beginning the stalemate on the Western Front was seen as a temporary phase, an aberration from the 'natural' forms of open warfare. But in striving to achieve a significant break in the opposing line the commanders failed to develop any new tactics. They relied upon old-style frontal infantry assaults and by their contempt for defensive firepower they were responsible for the horrifying casualty returns of the great set-piece battles. It was not that the generals were all fools; most of them had thought a great deal about modern warfare and they reckoned they had devised a scientific approach to conflict. But they had completely misunderstood the new technology that had become the dominant force on the battlefield.

To a large extent this blindness can be explained by the absolute importance of hierarchy and the inflexible reliance on seniority amongst the European officer corps at the turn of the century. Originality and initiative were stifled by respect for outmoded forms and procedures. Innovative younger officers were thwarted by the conservatism of their elders. For

in 1914 the High Commands were very much the preserve of the aristocracy; be they English 'milords', French noblemen or Prussian Junkers. Such men came from the very social group that had often been by-passed by the Industrial Revolution and the development of bourgeois democracy. Even among many of the new middle-class officers the ideals of the old aristocracies lingered on as the aspiring young subalterns found it expedient to adopt the conventions and condescending tones of their superiors.

Certain aspect of this class bias are merely trivial, such as the exaggerated emphasis upon tradition and custom, or the love of empty formalism. In France in 1912 one Colonel Maud'huy (in 1915 the commander of the 10th Army in

Field Marshal Sir John French, C in C in France with his ADCs at GHQ.

German General Staff at the
outbreak of the war.

Artois) announced to his assembled regiment: 'Many men
salute correctly, very rare are those who salute beautifully;
those latter are necessarily the ones who have achieved
complete suppleness and received a thorough physical and
moral instruction; they are the élite. One could say that the
salute is the hall-mark of education.' But such inanities of
petty ritualism had more serious implications in that they
extended to the very methods of fighting. For the officers of
1914 – still the commanders of 1918 – their conception of war
was based upon the memories of Waterloo or before. They
pictured, above all, a warfare in which man himself, *en masse*,
was the decisive element. They yearned for the glorious
charge, particularly by the cavalry, in which the courage and
impetus of man and beast was sufficient to bring victory. They
revered the bayonet and the *arme blanche* as a more than
adequate response to anything produced by the technological
revolution. Towards the end of the war a French soldier
expressed his loss of faith in just such a notion: 'Our men were
not driven on...by the chimera of glory – they died in
obscurity and unknown – nor by the assurance given in times
past by a strong arm and an intrepid heart – progress in
armaments had overwhelmed the valour of old.' Many of the
generals throughout the war never came to terms with this
complete change in the conduct of war. Though much was
written about military affairs in the years preceding World
War One, almost all of it consistently reveals a kind of military
'spiritualism', a continual stress upon human capabilities at
the expense of the potential of material forces.

Eighteenth and early nineteenth-century wars remained the
model. The lessons of later conflicts were resolutely ignored.
The American Civil War, it was held, had little to show about
what might happen in Europe. The lessons of more recent
conflicts, the Russo-Japanese and Boer Wars, both of which
demonstrated the new deadliness of infantry fire and the
necessity for entrenchments, were all forgotten. Even colonial
military experience was misinterpreted. When soldiers should

have been pondering upon the ghastly efficiency of the Gatlings at Ulundi, or the Maxims at Omdurman, they instead took the devastating casualties to be further proof of the black man's inferiority. Certainly few people thought such events were at all relevant in a 'civilised' European conflict.

Faith was in the man rather than the machine. In Britain, France and Germany all were agreed that moral qualities must be the final arbiter in battle. The French generals in particular were committed to the absolute pre-eminence of the offensive. Du Picq, with his emphasis upon morale, was one of the principle influences. In his *Etudes sur le combat* he wrote: 'In battle, two moral forces, even more so than two material forces [are in conflict].' And elsewhere: 'The human heart...is then the starting point in all matters pertaining to war...We shall learn...to distrust mathematics and material dynamics...to beware of the illusions drawn from the range and the manoeuvre field.' Such attitudes were dominant right up to 1914 and beyond. Foch, who in 1909 claimed that the Russo-Japanese War had no lessons to offer, said that 'A battle won is one in which one will not confess oneself to be beaten...To organise battle consists in enhancing our own spirit to the highest degree in order to break that of the enemy.

A 'stirrup charge' of the Scots Greys and Highlanders at St Quentin. One of the rare examples of how the strategists had thought the war was going to be fought.

The will to conquer: such is victory's primary condition.' Here is the essence of military 'spiritualism'. Joffre in 1912 said: 'The French Army, returning to its traditions, no longer knows any other law than that of the offensive... All attacks are to be pushed to the extreme with the firm resolution to charge the enemy with the bayonet, in order to destroy him.'

Though this mania for the offensive was expressed most forcefully, and notoriously, in French circles, it rested on assumptions common to all European military establishments. The Germans, too, grievously over-estimated the power of men in the face of new technology of death, even if they were a little more advanced than the French; von Schlieffen, for example, at least acknowledged that there was more to war than mere *élan*: 'A general's art is defined in that he must be numerically stronger on the battlefield.' But other very influential theorists like Bernhardi still fell back on the old assumptions: 'We must not overrate the importance of practical inventions for war, nor above all, imagine that mechanical appliances, be they ever so excellent, can make amends for deficiencies in military and moral qualities.' Of the offensive he wrote: 'There is *one* quality above all in man which is of the utmost importance in all warfare, and that really benefits the attack exclusively – boldness.'

Nor were British theories much different. Once again we find this constant harping on the moral superiority of the attack. One feature of this was a persistent faith in cavalry as the ultimate shock troops. In the early 1900s, Sir John French commented adversely on the behaviour of certain cavalry officers on manoeuvres: 'Umpires and officers try to inculcate such a respect for infantry fire that cavalry is taught to shirk exposure...We ought to be on our guard against false teachings of this nature...[and the] consequences of placing the weapon above the man.'Even in 1926, Sir Douglas Haig, who might have been expected to have learnt something about the limited applicability of cavalry in modern warfare, commented in a book review that: 'I believe that the value of the horse and the opportunity for the horse in the future are likely to be as great as ever...aeroplanes and tanks...are only accessories to the man and the horse, and I feel sure that as time goes on you will find just as much use for the horse – the well-bred horse – as you have ever done in the past.' The Cavalry Training Manual of 1907 perfectly summed up this faith in the superiority of the man to the machine: 'It must be accepted as a principle that the rifle, effective as it is, cannot replace the effect produced by the speed of the horse, the magnetism of the charge, and the terror of cold steel.'

The infantry too were to be allowed their participation in the 'magnetism of the charge', and for them also it was deemed decisive. On the general relation between attack and defence even so level-headed a military commentator as Spencer Wilkinson wrote:

It is true that within certain narrow limits...the defender is strengthened by modern improvements in firearms. But it is not true that this results in a great or sudden change in the relations of attack and defence...There has been no revolution in tactics or strategy...The balance of advantage remains where it was.

Thus the British Infantry Regulations are full of platitudes about the transcendent virtues of the attack and a mystical faith in its eventual success: 'The main essential to success is to close with the enemy, cost what it may. A determined and steady advance lowers the fighting spirit of the enemy...' Equally, though the effect of an attack might be influenced 'by the ground and the enemy's fire', the main determinant will

be 'the resolution and determination of the leaders in the front line'. The attack became the solution to all military problems. Another official textbook pronounced the unhelpful view that 'the most soldierly way out of what looks like an impossible situation is by an attack. The moral effect...even by a small force, is enormous.' As Sir William Robertson observed in 1910: 'The training regulations dealt with great persistence on the importance of the offensive, and the idea of fighting on the defensive was thought to be so obnoxious [that] it had been deemed politic to leave defensive training severely alone.'

German troops preparing to advance.

The basic tactical preconceptions of the First World War were simple, the most effective military technique was the attack, and the most useful weapon in such an attack was the morale, the superior dash and *élan* of the assaulting troops. It is this that made the offensives of the first years so horrendously bloody. In all wars the basic aim must be to attack eventually. But the art of generalship consists in deploying one's resources so that one achieves a favourable balance of forces. And of course the moral element is important. Successful guerrilla forces have always devoted much of their attention to the subversion of the enemy's 'will to resist'. Conventional generals have made much of the notions of 'surprise attacks' or the 'indirect approach', the basic aim of which is to catch the enemy off-balance and confused. Yet there is also a *material* balance of forces. There exist situations in which it is almost impossible for an attack to succeed simply because the disparity between the material force of the attacker and defender is too great. Crossbowmen

Armour plated sentry. Note the special reinforcement to his helmet.

and slow-moving knights could not face up to longbows. Thousands of Zulus, Matabeles or Dervishes could not make any headway against a few machine guns and rifles. In the 1920s and 1930s the Chinese Red Army could not storm cities. In the Western Desert the Afrika Korps could not match the material build-up of the Eighth Army. The point is so basic it is often overlooked. Before a commander can devise suitable tactics he must first appreciate the nature of the material balance. The generals of 1914 failed to do this. Because all the armies were organised and equipped in much the same way, it was thought that battles would be a close run thing in which victory would go to those that showed the greatest resolution, the greatest *will* to win. They completely ignored the implications of the weapons with which they had equipped themselves. They failed to see that when an army adopted a different role, when one attacked and one defended, there would be a vast disparity between the effectiveness of the available weaponry. Static machine guns and rifles must give almost the whole advantage to the defender. But the generals did not acknowledge this. For them the charge was a sort of limbo during which the defender nervously fingered his weapon, began to shake with fear and then simply bolted. Perhaps this conception had some validity a hundred years before. But in the trenches the defender was too sure of his weapons for this to be true. A German machine gunner looking over the sights of his Maxim, seeing the swathes of dead and dying, was more likely to pity his enemy's morale than to fear it.

A German Maxim crew on the Western Front during the first year of the war.

7 Battle: The Reality

And through some mooned Valhalla there will pass
Battalions and Battalions, scarred from hell;
The unreturning army that was youth;
The legions who have suffered and are dust.

Siegfried Sassoon

From the very first offensives, the primacy of defensive firepower in particular the machine gun was gruesomely apparent. Though artillery caused a great many casualties throughout the war, when advancing against the enemy trenches it was the machine gun bullet that was likely to fell a man. It is no exaggeration to say that they completely dominated the actual battlefield. The soldiers themselves very soon realised this. In 1914 a French Alpine Chasseur wrote:

> At the beginning of the war the Germans had more of them than we had, and every time a machine gun opened fire in our sector, my men would listen carefully, and when someone said, 'It's the coffee-mill', his remark would send a tingle down our spines... I know nothing more depressing in the midst of battle...than the steady tac-tac-tac of that deadly weapon...There appears to be nothing material to its working. It seems to be dominated and directed by some powerful, scheming spirit of destruction.

A young British officer told in a letter of the dreadful power of these weapons:

> They have plenty of machine guns, which, when properly handled can hold up armies. This is indeed no exaggeration and you would despair of ever making a big advance, especially with cavalry, if you could see the way in which troops are mown down by these little devils, worked by three brave men.

The Allied generals never did despair, however, of making such an advance. Time and time again, relying on little more than a mystical faith in the justice of their cause and the determination of their men, they threw troops forward against the wire and the Maxims. The point about faith is worth emphasising. Of course, any large offensive requires an inordinate amount of detailed staff work; prior to the Third Battle of Ypres the 2nd Northants had collected a file of orders that was fully one foot thick. But when it came to zero hour, the commanders seem to have been remarkably devoid of any substantive confidence in their arrangements. Writing in his diary on the eve of the Somme offensive, General Rawlinson was particularly vague:

What the actual result will be, none can say, but I feel pretty confident of success myself...That the Boche will break and that a debacle will supervene I do not believe, but should this be the case I am ready to take full advantage of it...The issues are in the hands of the Bon Dieu.

Before the disastrous Champagne offensive in April 1917, Nivelle showed greater confidence, but based it upon a quite vacuous mysticism:

The character of violence, of brutality and of rapidity must be maintained. It is in the speed and surprise caused by the rapid and sudden eruption of our infantry upon the third and fourth positions that the success of the rupture will be found. No consideration should intervene of a nature to weaken the *élan* of the attack.

Unfortunately barbed wire and machine guns would inevitably intervene. Impersonally, almost contemptuously, the most vigorous attacks were brushed aside. The casualty figures for the major offensives demonstrate all too clearly what became of *élan* and trust in God. Stephen Graham a Guards private in France brings out the most chilling aspect of these figures:

I do not know why the various occasions on which battalions have fought till there were merely a few score survivors have not been properly chronicled...Certain platoons or companies fought shoulder to shoulder till the last man dropped...or...were shelled to nothingness, or getting over the top...went forward till they all withered away under machine gun fire...A fortnight after some exploit, a field-marshal or divisional general comes down to a battalion to thank it for its gallant conduct, and fancies for a moment, perchance, that he is looking at the men who did the deed of valour, and not at a large draft that has just been brought up from England and the base to fill the gap. He should ask the services of the chaplain and make his congratulations in the grave-yard or go to the hospital and make them there.

In the first months of the war it was the French who sustained the heaviest casualties At Roselies near Charleroi on 22 August 1914, the 74th Infantry Regiment lost 1,100 men. At counter-attacks at St. Léonard-sur-Souche during the battle of Haute Meurthe in the following month, each of the attacking regiments lost an average of 800 men *killed*. In June 1915 during an attack in the Bagatelle sector in the Argonne, the 8th Battalion of Chasseurs was reduced to the colonel, three subalterns and less than 200 men. This unit was part of the

3rd Army and its commander, General Sarrail, wrote: 'Since the 8th January, I have lost in the Argonne, 1,200 officers and 82,000 men, almost a half of the Army's effective strength.'

But British casualties in 1915 were even more severe. During the Second Battle of Ypres in April 1915, whole brigades were almost annihilated. The 149th Brigade lost forty-two officers and 1,912 men, three-quarters of its complement, whilst the 10th Brigade virtually ceased to exist, losing seventy-three officers and 2,346 other ranks. Machine guns were largely responsible. The diary of the German 57th Regiment reads 'There could never before in war have been a more perfect target than this solid wall of khaki men...There was only one possible order to give: "Fire until the barrels burst."' At Neuve Chapelle in March 1915, the 2nd Middlesex was virtually wiped out by two German machine gun posts, which also caused many casualties in the adjoining 2nd Scottish Rifles with enfilade fire. At the Battle of Aubers Ridge in May fifteen German companies and twenty-two machine guns broke up an attack by three full brigades. In an attack by the 1st Battalion of the Black Watch only fifty men reached the German parapets alive. During the battle General Rawlinson complained to one of his Brigadier-Generals: 'This is most unsatisfactory. Where are the Sherwood Foresters? Where are the East Lancashires on the right?' Brigadier-General Oxley replied: 'They are lying out in no man's land, sir, and most of them will never stand again.' Even worse was the slaughter at the Battle of Loos in September. In the first two hours of the battle the British lost more men than were lost on the whole of D-Day 1945 by all three arms of the Services. The 15th Division lost sixty per cent of its men, and some of its battalions, the 9th Black Watch, the 8th Seaforth Highlanders, the 7th Cameron Highlanders and others, were almost completely destroyed. On the second day an attack was launched by twelve fresh battalions, a little under 10,000 men. In three and a half hours of fighting they lost 385 officers and 7,861 men. A German unit, the 15th Reserve Regiment, was quite clear about the main reason for such devastating casualties:

> Never had the machine gunners such straightforward work to do nor done it so effectively. They traversed to and fro along the enemy's ranks unceasingly. The men stood on the fire-steps, some even on the parapets, and fired triumphantly into the mass of men advancing across the open grassland. As the entire field of fire was covered with the enemy's infantry the effect was devastating and they could be seen falling literally in hundreds.

Exactly the same thing happened, on an even larger scale, along the Somme. A German machine gunner wrote of one unit:

At a single signal the entire 16 mile front of the British troops leap over their trench parapets to assault the German lines on the Somme. This amazing sequence of photographs was taken by one of the original wartime camera crews.

Bloated corpses left behind in no man's land in front of the Canadian lines.

We were very surprised to see them walking, we had never seen that before...The officers went in front. I noticed one of them walking calmly, carrying a walking stick. When we started firing we just had to load and reload. They went down in their hundreds. You didn't have to aim, we just fired into them.

The British themselves often simplified the Germans' task. To allow the troops to get into no man's land it was necessary to cut gaps in the wire just before the attack. As one soldier who was there remarked: 'The advertisement of the attack on our front was absurd. Paths were cut and marked...days before...Small wonder the machine gun fire was directed with such fatal precision.' The casualties on the first day of the Somme, 1 July 1916, were particularly horryfying. Two whole brigades of the 8th Division were mown down by the German machine gunners around Ovillers. In little more than two hours the Division lost 218 of its 300 officers and 5,274 of its 8,500 other ranks. The German defenders lost just under 300 men. In front of Fricourt two whole battalions, the 10th West Yorkshires and the 7th Green Howards, were almost completely destroyed by one well-sited Maxim. In front of 'Y' Ravine the Newfoundland Regiment tried to advance into the machine guns. As they crossed the few hundred yards of no man's land 710 men fell. Edmund Blunden later recalled his impressions of the Somme Battle:

We come to wire which is uncut, and beyond we see grey coal-scuttle helmets bobbing about... and the loud crackling of machine-guns changes to a screeching as of steam being blown off by a hundred engines, and soon no-one is left standing.

Nor should one suppose that all these horrors were concentrated into just one single day. Officially the Battle of the Somme went on for a further five months and scenes like these occurred time and time again. For the first three days of the battle the average casualties per division were 101 officers and 3,320 men. During the whole of the second week the British were losing 10,000 men, an entire division, per day and for the remainder of the battle the daily average was 2,500 men. The great British offensive of the following year produced similar losses. During the Third Battle of Ypres from August to November, attack after attack was broken up by the German machine gunners: a total of 244,897 men were killed or wounded. Yet despite the slaughter that the men knew awaited them when they went over the top discipline held. On arrival at the jumping-off trenches, where each battalion's position was marked out by tapes laid the previous day, they waited stoically for the signal to advance. All that could be heard was the deafening artillery barrage, making the trenches rock and crumble. Just before the attack a rum ration would be issued. Though the rum was potent the amount given to each man was strictly limited and the effect was little more than that of a whisky after some nasty shock. With most of the men keyed up for the coming assault, the alcohol tended to sharpen their senses rather than to deaden them. A Canadian private wrote of the prelude to the attack on Vimy Ridge:

German stormtroopers carry French positions.

I have had people ask me if it was true that before we went into battle we got well soaked with rum. Well we got one stiff tot after struggling to reach the firing step of the take-off trench...and it has very little effect on any man after the night march.

With or without the rum each soldier was keenly aware of his own fears and hopes. Each tried to come to terms with the fact that in a few minutes he was quite likely to be killed or horribly maimed. In the daily routine of the trenches one could convince oneself that the odds were very much against being hit by a chance shell or a sniper's bullet and that one could reduce the odds even further by not taking unnecessary risks. But once over the top, one was completely exposed. The bullets and shells were just as likely to hit you as anyone else.

British troops leave from a sap to attack the German positions on the Somme.

So each man waited, saying very little as he wrestled with his own fears, wondering if his neighbours felt the same way. A Scottish private wrote: 'The fifteen minutes before "going over" have a peculiar eeriness all their own. One's heart seems to thump a little louder, while a pulse in the throat keeps beating in unison with it...As the zero hour approaches...we are left with nothing to take our minds off the dragging minutes.' This sense of utter self-absorption is emphasised by an English soldier:

The skin seemed shinier and tighter on men's faces, and eyes burned with a hard brightness under the brims of their helmets. One felt every question as an interruption of some absorbing business of the mind...One by one, they realised that each must go alone, and that each of them already was alone with himself, helping the others perhaps, but looking at them with strange eyes, while the world became unreal and empty, and they moved in a mystery, where no help was.

Yet it was the presence of one's comrades, the sense of being an insignificant part of the unit as a whole, that gave men their basic motivation at such a time. Every instinct screamed at one to stay where one was, to hide, to run back. One was acutely conscious of oneself as a living body, horribly

Canadians fix bayonets in readiness for a charge.

vulnerable yet with its own sacrosanct destiny. One had one's family, one's friends, one's expectations, one's dreams. Surely it was madness to risk all this in a mad dash across no man's land? A French sergeant described this agonising consciousness of the physical self prior to an attack at Verdun:

> To be able to comport oneself correctly in the fact of death. It's not very difficult to say this little phrase; but, my God, what a terrible effort it demands! What a hideous thing; to say to oneself, at this moment I am myself; my blood circulates and pulses in my arteries; I have my eyes, all my skin is intact, I do not bleed!...Oh to be able to sleep thinking that it is finished, that I shall live, that I shall not be killed!

But dominating everything was the key notion of 'comporting oneself correctly'. A man might not, at such a moment, be conscious of the other men as individuals, but there was always at the back of his mind the fear of their collective contempt, their feeling of betrayal if he allowed himself to panic. Each man struggled with his intense private fears and nearly all triumphed simply because they would rather be dead than be revealed to their fellows as cowards. The battle was within oneself, but collective opinion was decisive. As one officer wrote: 'The honour of my battalion and its opinion of me. These are now my sustaining motives in the game of war.' A British captain summed up the never-ending sense of self-doubt that nagged at men's minds: 'We are not ashamed of being afraid, as we often are – not afraid of anything definite thing, but just afraid of being afraid.' For most men these torments were muted by a sudden pleasure in the realisation that, come what may, they *would* be able to go through with it, they would be able to force themselves over the top. A.G. West explained how central were his doubts about his own abilities:

I don't definitely *fear* the infliction of pain or wound...It is the knowledge that something may happen with which one will not be able to cope or that one's old resolutions of courage, etc., will fail in this new set of experiences...One may be called upon to bear or perform something to which one will find oneself inadequate.

A French officer recalled a typical new recruit waiting to go forward:

Moreau, come here. There you have a brave young chap. It was his first 'show'. He was sweating with fear, shaking with fear. Yes, yes, I saw you. He nearly fell down when he went over. He gripped his rifle, he threw himself forward, he yelled as if to deafen himself; and he went because he had to go. He was afraid of nothing so much as showing his fear.

An NCO of the 22nd Manchester Rifles wrote of his experiences during the Battle of the Somme:

I hadn't gone ten yards before I felt a load fall from me...I had been worried by the thought: 'Suppose one should lose one's head and get other men cut up! Suppose one's legs should take fright and refuse to move!' Now I knew it was all right. I shouldn't be frightened and I shouldn't lose my head. Just imagine the joy of that discovery! I felt quite happy and self-possessed.

Most accounts of men's experiences in assaults agree that the feeling of fear vanished as soon as they went over the top. The barrage would stop, or move further forward, the officers

would blow their whistles, and everyone clambered up the
ladders and dashed forward. Few men can remember clearly
what happened after that. One abiding impression is of utter
confusion. All units had carefully delineated objectives, but
when the moment came it was impossible to maintain the
correct direction, or even to know whether the objective had
actually been reached. Even those watching a battle from a
distance were rarely able to make out what was happening.
Guy Chapman wrote of an attack at Arras: 'The story of this
attack will no doubt appear in the military history of the war,
elucidated by diagrams. To the watchers on the hill-side it
was only a confused medley, in which English and Germans
appeared most disconcertingly, going to and fro, oblivious of
each other.'

In the attack itself, the officers tried desperately to keep
their men together, pointing the right way; the men tried to
keep up with their neighbours and pay attention to the

commands of their officers and NCOs; all struggled to avoid the shell-holes, to drag their feet through the mud or to disentangle themselves from the barbed wire. All this left little time to feel afraid. Alan Thomas has tried to describe his feelings:

> We climbed up our ladders and went forward. It was a strange sensation walking upright in no man's land when up till then you had only crawled. But I did not feel afraid, or at least not nearly so afraid as I had felt immediately before going over...But now there was so much to think about, so much to distract my attention, that I forgot to feel afraid – it is the only explanation. The noise, the smoke, the smell of gunpowder, the rat-tat of rifle and machine gun fire combined to numb the senses. I was aware of myself and others going forward, but of little else.

Another soldier, Patrick McGill of the London Irish, who took part in the Battle of Loos, has also drawn attention to this lack of fear. His remarks are a further indication of the way in which membership of a battalion *obliged* one to go forward, irrespective, almost, of any concern for one's personal safety:

> The moment had come when it was unwise to think...To dwell for a moment on the novel position of being standing where a thousand deaths swept by, missing you by a mere hairsbreadth would be sheer folly. There on the open field of death my life was out of my keeping, but the sensation of fear never entered my being. There was so much simplicity and so little effort on doing what I had done, in doing what eight hundred comrades had done, that I felt I could carry through the work before me with as much credit as my code of self-respect required.

Not only did most men not feel fear, it is difficult to find evidence of any particular conscious thought at all. Carrington found that he became almost schizophrenic, the urge for self-preservation oscillating wildly with a fey eagerness for battle:

> Through these days of battle one lived in an elevated state of mind which a doctor might have defined as a neurosis. The strange sense of dual personality...was hardly ever absent. There was an arguing realism, a cynical side to one's nature that raised practical objections and suggested dangers, and against it there strove a romantic ardour for the battle that was almost joyful...Always the struggle within, fought behind the dark curtains which screen the hidden springs of conduct, was more real than the physical struggle without, and the practical details of life passed by like an illusion.

Many others shared this sense of illusion. To those going forward everything around them seemed strangely unreal, and they saw it, if at all, only as indifferent observers. Having come to terms with their fears and forced themselves over the top, the men gladly immersed themselves in the collective activity of their unit, and completely abandoned their powers of independent observation and assessment. Once the dread of the future became an ongoing reality the soldiers felt as though what they did was done independently of their own volition. Alexander Aitken took part in an attack at Goose Alley during the Battle of the Somme in September 1916:

'I passed through the smoke...In an attack such as this, under deadly fire, one is as powerless as a man gripping strongly charged electrodes, powerless to do anything but go mechanically on; the final shield from death removed, the will is fixed like the last thought taken into an anaesthetic, which is the first thought taken out of it. Only safety, or the shock of a wound will destroy such auto-hypnosis. At the same time all normal emotion is numbed utterly.

British soldiers scramble out of their battered trench.

Other soldiers have described the feeling of unreality that was so strong during an assault. A soldier of the Queen's Westminster Rifles, who took part in an attack on Gommecourt in 1916, described his feelings in the third person:

> Horden stumbled blindly forwards across no man's land. It seemed to him that he was alone in a pelting storm of machine gun bullets, shell fragments and clods of earth. Alone, because the other men were like figures on a cinematograph screen – an old film that flickered violently – everybody in a desperate hurry – the air full of black rain. He could recognise some of the figures in an uninterested way. Some of them stopped and fell down slowly. The fact that they had been killed did not penetrate his intelligence...They were unreal to him. His mind was numbed by noise, the smoke, the dust.

A private of the Royal Welsh Fusiliers, attacking Mametz Wood, felt much the same way:

> It was life rather than death that faded away into the distance, as I grew into a state of not-thinking, not-feeling, not-seeing. I moved past trees, past other things; men passed by me, carrying other men, some crying, some cursing, some silent. They were all shadows, and I was no greater than they. Living or dead, all were unreal...Past and future were equidistant and unattainable, throwing no bridge of desire across the gap that separated me from my remembered self and from all that I had hoped to grasp.

In hardly any of the personal accounts of the Western Front are men able to give a lucid description of what they or their units actually accomplished during an attack. Enervated by the effort of screwing themselves up in the minutes before zero hour, their senses numbed by the deafening racket around them, caught up unthinkingly in the corporate rush forwards, the troops were more like zombies devoid of their everyday feelings of fear, squeamishness or compassion. No abstract concepts *persuaded* them to go forwards; nor did rational calculations make them deem it wise to turn back. They were caught up in the sheer momentum of the forward rush; an unthinking mass pushing forward until they were literally annihilated by the insuperable density of the opposing firepower. This irrelevance of the individual, in terms of the actual battles, was expressed by Guy Chapman in a moving valediction to an anonymous infantryman: 'Hump your pack and get a move on. The next hour, man, will bring you three miles nearer your death. Your life and your death are nothing to these fields – nothing, no more than it is to the man

The second wave at Arras.

planning the next attack at GHQ. You are not even a pawn.'

Nor, at the time, did the soldiers concern themselves much with the impact of their individual contribution to the war. For the time being, to have survived an attack was enough. Few thought back on what they had done with any idea of relating it to conventional platitudes about duty, heroism, patriotism or religion. Such notions were important in bringing men to France in the first place, and in sustaining them during the tormenting months of ordinary trench warfare. But reactions after battle were simply those of men utterly exhausted, yet glad to be alive. It became customary amongst British writers to interview the survivors of the bigger battles to produce stirring copy for those back home. Speaking of the supposed accounts of the Somme veterans, one officer wrote: 'These preposterous storie were read and laughed at by every soldier in the line and were considered an immense joke.' One of the few writers whose reports seem to ring true was John Masefield. One man who had just emerged from an attack on the Somme told him:

> I tried to tell myself that I was doing it for this or that reason, to make it sound better, but I didn't believe those grand things. When you are waiting to be killed those damned newspapers seem damned thin, and so do those damned poems about the Huns. The Fritzes are a dirty lot, but they are damned brave you may say what you like. And being killed by a lot of damned Fritzes is damned bad egg, and no amount of talk will alter it.

Some seem to have made a deliberate point of deglorifying their exploits. After an attack at Verdun a French soldier, Raymond Joubert, savagely probed his own reactions:

> What sublime emotion inspires you at the moment of assault? I thought of nothing other than dragging my feet out of the mud encasing them. What did you feel after surviving the attack? I grumbled because I would have to remain several days more without *pinard* [wine]. Is not one's first act to kneel down and thank God? No. One relieves oneself.

8 The Casualties

Who are these? Why sit they here in twilight?
Wherefore rock they, purgatorial shadows?
Drooping tongues from jaws that slob their relish,
Baring teeth that leer like skulls' teeth wicked? Stroke on stroke of
pain - but what slow panic,
Gouged these chasms round their fretted sockets?
And from their hair and through their hands' palms
Misery swelters. Surely we have perished
Sleeping, and walk in hell; but who these hellish?

Wilfred Owen

Even in the bloodiest offensives, the odds were against one being killed. In a day's battle, the percentage of men killed outright was never more than thirty per cent, often much less. For the war as a whole, on the Western Front the British lost 118,941 officers and 2,571,113 men as battle casualties, of whom a quarter were killed. Over half the British soldiers suffered some kind of wound in battle – a clear indication that the medical services were not just there to serve a few unfortunates, but were as integral a part of the front line soldier's life as the ration parties or his own officers.*

The first problem for any man wounded in an attack was to get any attention at all. Advancing troops were usually forbidden to stop and care for wounded comrades and often they were not even aware that a friend had been hit. All men carried an emergency field-dressing which, if they were able to, they might apply to their wound. Then there was nothing to do but wait for the stretcher-bearers. In the chaos of battle, and with so many men to care for, a lot were missed. Some wounded lay for two or three days before they were picked up or, what was more likely, died. Some dragged themselves into a shell-hole for protection, and then slowly drowned as they sank into the mud. Sometimes, after a patrol, or if an attack were beaten back, the wounded would lie very close to their own trenches. Their position was easily pin-pointed because of their cries and pleas for help, but it was usually impossible to send anyone out after them. Such men were simply left to die, and soldiers within earshot could come to hate those who took so long to die. Each scream or moan was a constant indictment of one's own determination to stay alive and a torturing reminder that next time it might be oneself. Some men survived for incredibly long periods and were eventually brought back to their own lines. A physician with the Royal Army Medical Corps, W. Herringham, came across several such cases. An officer hit in the chest during the Battle of Loos lived in a shell-hole for four days, keeping himself alive with the rain-water he was able to catch in his cap. A private with a broken leg was not found for a week. Another with a broken thigh spent two days dragging himself backwards with his hands, until he reached his own trenches. A soldier shot through the chest at Arras remained near the German lines for eleven days and nights until the Germans found him. Amazingly, all these men eventually recovered.

Normally there were only four stretcher-bearers per

*The French suffered 3,926,000 battle casualties (including men captured) out of a total of 6,300,000 mobilised troops (62 per cent). The Germans, on both fronts, had 1,733,000 men killed out of a total of 11,000,000 called up. The American figures are rather misleading. They suffered 322,000 battle casualties, of whom 115,000 were killed, out of a total force of 2,039,329. But, although all these latter arrived in Europe, a large proportion of them never actually reached the front before the German collapse.

company, and even when extra men were brought in from units in reserve or the RAMC field ambulances they were often completely overwhelmed by their task. In theory it needed two men to carry each wounded man. In actual fact, appalling physical conditions often meant that two were completely inadequate. Herringham noted that at Beaumont Hamel in November 1916 and at Passchendaele, it took four men to lift a stretcher and ten to carry it more than a short distance. The effort of dragging one's feet out of the mud at every step, whilst trying not to disturb the wounded man too much, was utterly fatiguing. Harold Chapin, an RAMC corporal, wrote to his mother in May 1915: 'I gave a hand with my party of six and between us we carried down two: you have no idea of the physical fatigue entailed in carrying a twelve stone *blessé* a thousand odd yards across muddy fields.' Even when the weather was reasonably good, transporting wounded men was still a trying business. At some stage they had to be carried through the trenches to the front-line aid

At least four men were normally needed to carry one through the mud.

post or beyond. Negotiating the bends and traverses of a trench with a six-foot stretcher, carrying a man to whom every jolt might be agony, was no simple task at the best of times. With men constantly coming the other way, others trying to hustle past from behind, it could become a herculean task. Bearers often had to inch their way forward with the stretcher held above their heads. One described a typical journey from the battlefield at Thiepval, in 1916:

> The trenches were knee-deep in glueing mud and it was the hardest work I have ever done...The banks on each side were full of buried and half-buried corpses and the stench was appalling. As one was carrying a wounded man down, one perhaps got stuck in the mud and staggered whilst one extricated oneself or was extricated. You put out a hand to steady yourself, the earth gave way and you found that you were clutching the blackened face of a half-buried German.

The sights these stretcher-bearers had to immure themselves to were horrific. Bullets usually made fairly clean wounds, unless a man was hit by a ricochet, in which case the bullet might strike end on and tear a hole in the chest or smash the face to pulp. But many of the wounds were caused by shell and grenade fragments, with ghastly results. The flying splinters might take off an arm or a leg. They might almost miss as they went between your legs but leave you neatly castrated. Some men lost an ear in this way, others their nose. Men might be found in no man's land still alive, even semi-conscious, with the lower half of their face sliced off or the top of their head and their brains clearly visible. Men arrived still breathing at the regimental aid posts with holes the size of a football between their shoulder-blades. Doctors might gently prise apart the hands of a man clutching his midriff and recoil, sickened, as his intestines spilled out over his trousers.*

Once he had been picked up by the stretcher-bearers, the wounded men would be taken first to the regimental aid post. This was usually in the second or third line of trenches, in a dugout or cellar, and was run by a regimental medical officer. Here wounds were diagnosed, dressings changed or rearranged and certain injections given. Only in the most desperate cases, usually those calling for amputation, was any actual surgery attempted. The aim was to get a man to the

---

*Out of one sample of just under 50,000 men admitted to Casualty Clearing Stations (CCSs), twenty-three per cent were wounded by bullets and the rest by shells and grenades. In both cases the most likely places to be hit were the head and neck, the arms above the elbow or the legs and thighs. Between them these areas accounted for sixty per cent of bullet wounds and fifty-three per cent of those from shells. Chest wounds seem to have been surprisingly low, probably because the wounded died before they reached the aid station.

Company dogs with first aid and stimulants off to search for the wounded in no man's land.

rear as soon as possible. In fact some writers have claimed that the regimental doctors were largely wasted. Unable to cope with the influx of casualties during a battle, such trained personnel might have been more effectively used in the hospitals themselves, leaving trained orderlies to do the work in the aid posts. It is certainly true that their forward position involved a terrible drain on manpower. During the war, over 1,000 British and 1,500 German medical officers were killed.

On leaving the aid post the wounded soldier was taken by bearer to an Advanced Dressing Station where again little surgery was attempted. Unless there was a need to control a haemorrhage, remove a smashed limb, or give initial treatment for gas poisoning, the patient was again sent on his way as quickly as possible, either by motor ambulance or ambulance train. His next destination was a Casualty Clearing Station and it was in these that most of the surgery was done. These CCSs were fairly extensive units. On average they had six operating tables, and a maximum daily capacity of 2,000 patients. There was one for each division, though they remained in the same place, serving different divisions as they came into the line. In the first months of the war, the CCS was usually situated in an actual building, but by the time of the Battle of the Somme the buildings had been destroyed by shell fire and canvas and portable huts were used. But this should

not belie the fact there was a marked improvement in the conditions in the CCSs. Early in the war the medical services were almost overwhelmed. No motor ambulances had been provided, which caused terrible delays and congestion when trying to get the wounded back. Conditions in the hospitals themselves were at best primitive. Even trestle beds were not provided until March 1915. Before that, as one nurse wrote: 'There were only stretchers with brown blankets laid on bare floors – no trolleys or dressing tables; an empty petrol can for soiled dressings, and a piece of clean paper as a tray for fresh dressings.' But as the war stabilised and the authorities began to come to terms with the massive demands made on the medical services, the situation gradually began to improve. The number of beds was drastically increased, as was the number of medical personnel. In 1914 the RAMC was made of 20,000 Regulars and Territorials. By 1918 there were 13,000 officers alone and more than 150,000 other ranks. Nurses too came to France in ever-increasing numbers. They were not allowed to go nearer the front than the CCS and their relations with the men were so circumscribed that they were formally forbidden even to dance. Nevertheless they were of immense psychological importance. Suffering became bearable with the prospect of a woman's soothing words and gentle touch. The realisation that life was not just a mud-hole,

RAMC field dressing station.

that gentleness and compassion still existed, could make even the prospect of death less hideous.

In fact, for most men at the front the hospitals were their only link with normality. Not only did they offer the almost forgotten luxuries of cleanliness and good food, but they were the only gateway through which one might permanently escape the agonies of the trenches. There were few men who did not dream of receiving a wound that, though not bad enough to kill, ensured one's being invalided out of the army. Talk in the trenches came back again and again to the legendary 'blighty one' or 'jammy one', and the chances of being crippled or disfigured were gladly reckoned with as long as it meant escape from the line. For the French such a wound was known as *une 'bonne' blessure*. Lieutenant Arnaud described how some of his men 'were struck by bursting shells. I admired the way in which, in a trice, they dumped their packs, equipment and rifles and feverishly strode off... towards the rear, towards life.' Sometimes men were cruelly deceived. A Territorial writing home in 1915 described a wounded man in his platoon: 'At first he rejoiced at having got a "blighty one". Gradually...he seemed to know that he would not see his home again. Before the end his blasphemies rang out in the morning air. It is evidently very hard to die to the song of the lark.'

In the first moths of the war, particularly, many men died from wounds that should not have proved fatal. The main causes were either shock or what was known as gas gangrene. Shock was particularly prevalent amongst those who received a serious wound in the thigh, known to the doctors as GSW femur. When such a case was being transported the pain of the shattered bone ends grating together was so intense that men often fell into a fatal coma. The patient would become very pale, his pupils dilated. His skin would become cold and clammy to the touch and beads of sweat would appear on his forehead. The only way to bring such a case round was to keep him very warm. All the medical staffs developed a process known as *rechauffement,* in which some sort of heater was placed under the man's bed and blankets draped over him reaching to the floor. Men wounded in the thorax or the abdomen were also very prone to shock, though occasionally it could affect someone with the most trivial scratch. On balance it was found that young men were more prone than the experienced veterans.

Gas gangrene was an even deadlier phenomenon, and it was here that the most important medical advances of the war were made. The term has nothing to do with poison gas. The condition had its origin in the nature of the soil in France and Flanders. Because it was so heavily cultivated it was also full of manure. This manure contained a bacillus that normally resides in a horse's intestines. In the trenches a man's clothes

Blinded Australians lying
out in the open at an aid post.

became impregnated with these bacilli. When he was hit by a
bullet or a shell fragment, portions of his uniform would be
driven into the wound and it would become infected. A doctor
at the front described the ensuing symptoms:

> After forty-eight hours the edges of the wound begin to
> swell up and turn...making it gape...The cut surface takes
> on a curious half-jellified, half-mummified look; then the
> whole wounded limb begins to swell up and distend in the
> most extraordinary fashion, turning, as it does so, first an
> ashy white and then a greenish colour. This is because the
> tissues are being literally blown out with gas, and on
> pressing the fingers down on this balloon-like swelling, a
> distinct crackling or tiny bubbling sensation can be felt.

At first doctors felt that such wounds ought to be left alone,
somehow to cure themselves. But as the fatalities mounted
different methods were clearly called for. A French surgeon,

Carrel, began to take immediate preventive surgery and to remove all tissue in and around the wound that might become infected. After this the open wound was constantly irrigated with a saline solution that would prevent any reinfection. By the end of the war his methods had been widely adopted and deaths from gangrene were drastically reduced.

But no matter what improvements were made in medical techniques and facilities, a CCS was always a nightmarish place in which to work. The strain on the nerves caused by a constant stream of dying and mutilated men could become almost unbearable. An officer wrote of the ward in which he was a patient: 'There were about twenty of us, and the noise of the groans was fairly continuous. I was glad of this, because I found groaning eased my breathing and I was able to do so without attracting attention. [The sister] seemed almost unreal...in all that bedlam. Fellows calling out in their delirium. One shouted "Charge" at the top of his voice.' Reverend Walker, a padre at a CCS during the Battle of the Somme, was almost overwhelmed by the sights he was compelled to confront each day:

> It is a good thing not to be too squeamish, the smell of septic limbs and heads is enough to bowl one over. As usual a good many deaths, one had the back of his head off, another from the nose downwards completely gone. But it is the multiple wounds that appear worst, men almost in pieces, the number intensifies the horror, we get so few slight cases.

Doctors, too, wearied not only of the endless round of chopping off shattered limbs and sewing up ripped flesh, but of the constant need to be optimistic, to assure a dying man that he would pull through, or make light of the most devastating surgery. One surgeon, Harold Dearden, told of a typical case:

> The lad was very good when I told him I thought he'd better have it off, but he looked straight ahead of him and said nothing – just looked with his poor thin nostrils working like a rabbit's, and shooting a dry, dirty tongue out every few seconds to moisten his gluey lips. I don't think he heard many of the lies I told him about men who could do anything with an artificial leg that they could do before, but there is really nothing else you can say.

The worst of all was to watch men dying, knowing that nothing could be done, yet trying to reassure them, listening sympathetically to their almost incoherent mumblings. Most of Harold Chapin's letters home are full of inconsequential trivia, showing his determination to hide the reality from his wife and mother. Yet occasionally he is forced to reveal something of his emotional distress. In a letter to his mother, written shortly before his death at Loos, he refers, almost apologetically to his love for his family and compares it with his

...very fresh recollections of men who have died near me – their little collections of letters and photos – their weakening, wearying oft, talks about their home people, their chums out here, and how they got their wounds – their gentle deliria in which it all came out again this time more freely – sometimes in the first or second person instead of narratively in the first and third – sometimes even in a strange medley of narrative and dialogue, objective and subjective, sometimes sung to tuneless chants, sometimes to popular melodies.

A nurse in France, Sister Luard, also recalled hearing the dying words of so many soldiers. One instance she cites in her memoirs, which she remembered as the most poignant thing she heard during her service, were the last words of a twenty-year-old Londoner, spoken in May 1916:

I fought I was too big to be walkin' about the street wivout joinin'...I fought a lot of fings when that shell hit...I fought about...going over the water again...and I fought about seein' Mother...And I fought about dyin'. Will they let her come and see me quick when I get to a hospital in London? I fink I'll write to her this afternoon.

'Dear Mother — this hospital is tres bon, and the nurses are angels.' Note the bottle of Guinness on the left to give the man strength.

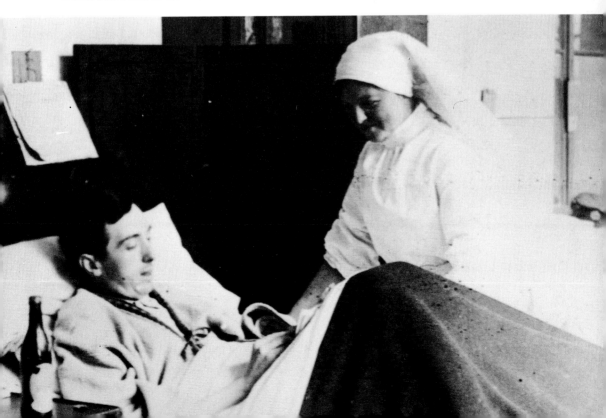

This one faltering speech can stand for all the tragedy of the Western Front. Yet despite the thousands of personal tragedies, most wounded men did not die. Only seven per cent of those passing through the aid posts and Advanced Dressing Stations died; in the CCSs the figure was sixteen per cent, in the Base Hospitals even further back a mere six per cent. Many men actually made a full recovery. Of all the millons of sick and wounded, a full seventy-eight per cent were returned to active service. One is entitled to ask, however, how 'full' many of these recoveries were. Men who had contracted trench foot were sent back with various toes missing. During the great offensives the lot of the sick was very hard, as the hospitals were cleared to make room for the battle casualties. Men with scabies and similar complaints were returned to the line at Saulcourt in March 1918. In the previous year, one doctor wrote home: 'Our medical arrangements are strange nowadays; it seems customary to return a man to duty, who is suffering from a heart or pulmonary tuberculosis. Unless the "Power" can *spot* it, a man has nothing serious the matter with him.'

In mid-1916 the authorities began to feel that one owed the wounded something more than just another chance to get killed. So for every wound received one was allowed to sew a stripe on one's sleeve. A scale of cash payments was also drawn up. The maximum payment, for a full year away from duty, was £250. But there were many men who never received a wound stripe or a gratuity, and yet who had suffered as much as any physical casualty. These were the 'shell-shock' cases, the psychological casualties of the war. The vagueness of the term accurately reflects the uncertainty of official policy towards these men. For many generals, and even doctors, most victims of shell-shock were little more than cowards and malingerers who simply ought to 'pull themselves together' and 'act like a man'. The term covered two quite dissimilar types of case. On the one hand there were those who were caught in a shell-burst and either blown in the air or buried alive. For them it was possible to make some kind of physical diagnosis. A bursting shell creates a vacuum, and when the air rushes into this vacuum it disturbs the cerebro-spinal fluid and this in turn can upset the working of the brain. But other cases were quite different. C.S. Meyers was at one stage in charge of psychological treatment in France and he wrote:

A shell...may play no part whatever in the causation of 'shell-shock': excessive emotion, e.g. sudden horror or fear – indeed any 'physical trauma' or 'inadjustable experience' – is sufficient. Morever, in men already worn out or having previously suffered from the disorder, the final cause of the breakdown may be so slight, and its onset so gradual, that its origin hardly deserves the name of 'shock'. 'Shell-shock', therefore, is a singularly ill-chosen term.

Tentative efforts were made to distinguish between the various types of cases. One typology split up neurasthenic cases and those regarded as hysteric. The former displayed chronic symptoms which gradually intensified – tiredness, irritability, giddiness, inability to concentrate, headaches. Their worries were on a conscious level, whereas the hysteric would suddenly break down as a reaction to subconscious, repressed fears. But this was never more than a very loose distinction. For many their complaint was never defined any more precisely than NYD(N). Not Yet Diagnosed (Nervous).

The sheer number of these cases forced the authorities to take action; though it can hardly be said that they threw themselves wholeheartedly into the problem. Dr. Meyers related that, throughout the war: 'In the RAMC...I never met with a regular officer who had any specialist's training or experience in mental or nervous diseases or disorders'. But some specialists were recruited on a temporary basis and

Shell-shock

special hospitals were set up to deal with this kind of case. By late 1916 each British Corps had two Divisional Rest Stations, each with provision for 500 to 1,000 men. Soldiers stayed there for about two weeks on average, during which time they were well fed, at first allowed to rest completely and then put on a programme of graduated exercises. These special Rest Stations were mainly intended to forestall the extreme symptoms of shell-shock and officers tended to have priority. There was much less sympathy for a ranker who looked or felt as though he *might* 'crack up', because, in theory at least, there were no other people relying upon his continued competence. The ordinary soldier usually had to endure until his breakdown actually occurred, and even then he might be merely shunted off into some carefully partitioned Bedlam. Jeffrey Farnol was once being shown round a Base Hospital when they came across what the doctor blithely referred to as the 'mad ward'. Farnol described a room full of men with 'a vagueness of gaze, a loose-lipped, too-ready smile, a vacancy of expression. Some there were who scowled sullenly enough, others who crouched apart, solitary souls, who, I learned, felt themselves outcast: others who crouched in corners haunted by the dread of a pursuing vengeance always at hand.' Philip Gibbs also saw such cases, such as the sergeant-major in Aveluy Wood, near Thiepval, who was 'convulsed with a dreadful rigor like a man in epilepsy, and clawed at his mouth, moaning horribly, with blind terror in his eyes. He had to be strapped to a stretcher before he could be carried away.' In almost the same place he saw a Wiltshire boy standing outside a dugout:

> Shaking in every limb, in a palsied way. His steel hat was at the back of his head, and his mouth slobbered, and two comrades could not hold him still. These badly shell-shocked boys clawed their mouths ceaselessly. It was a common, dreadful action. Others sat in the field hospitals in a state of coma, dazed, as though deaf, and actually dumb.

On shell-shock cases the records are very incomplete, particularly for the years 1915 and 1916. But the Medical History of the War made the rather smug extrapolation from what figures do exist that total wastage from shell-shock was not much more than two per cent – 80,000 cases. Presumably one either takes comfort from the fact that only one man in fifty could not 'take it', or wonders at a situation where 80,000 men were driven temporarily or permanently insane.

But there is more than this to make the complacency of the Medical History so out of place. For their figure of 80,000 is, to say the least, somewhat arbitrary. Shell-shock was not something one either had or did not have, like measles or a broken leg. It was an extreme point along a steady progression of emotional torment. Simply because one did not finally 'break down' did not mean that one was not suffering intense anguish. Even the authorities themselves had no clear idea of what was enough to constitute shell-shock. One chaplain served at a reception centre for such cases at Mondicourt, during the Battle of the Somme. The staff were almost overwhelmed and, as he says: 'Later on a much stricter rule was enforced as to who might be considered to be suffering from genuine shock. It is interesting to note that in one sample of 28,533 cases of shell-shock between September 1914 and December 1917, 16,138 were admitted between July and December 1916, the period of the Somme battles. The figure for July to December 1917, embracing the Third Battle of Ypres, is only 4,938. Are we to assume that men were suddenly more capable of standing up to the strain or, that the symptoms had to be much more acute before a diagnosis for shock was made?

The statistics then are not a reliable guide to the extent of emotional strain. Many men who were never officially classified as being shell-shocked from time to time began to feel that their self-control was slipping away. H. Quigley of the 12th Royal Scots remembered the war as 'that time of emotional stress and unequalled difficulty of retaining mental stability.' Another officer remembered that: 'My nerves went to pieces in direct ratio to the length of my stay at the front.' Julian Tyndale-Biscoe was a lieutenant in the Royal Horse Artillery, eighteen years old when the following incident occurred:

When sitting with Chadwick in our mess I suddenly felt a queer attack of cold feet coming on for no reason at all. I told Chadwick...that if the Bosche should pitch some shells over, I would run like a hare. Almost immediately a salvo came over...Off I went like a long-dog, with Chadwick, who had obviously been affected by my nerves, close behind. Out we ran into the rain, laughing quite uncontrollably and falling into shell holes, until we sort of sobered up.

In a typical offensive men would have to go over the top time and time again, attacking, fighting off counter-attacks, being shelled, receiving neither water nor food, nor being able to take more than a few minutes sleep for days at a time. It is only surprising that everyone did not go stark mad. Henry Williamson was on the Somme and he saw what happened to men forced to go into such a maelstrom. He has described them as they limped back from the front line:

Men, single and in couples, shuffling past them, answering no questions...men without rifles, haggard, bloodshot-eyed, slouching past in loose file, slouching on anywhere,

anyhow, staggering under rifles and equipment, some with haws sagging, puttees coiled mud-boiled around ankles, feet in shapeless mud boots, swelled beyond feeling, men slouching on beyond fatigue and hope, on and on and on...Stretcher-bearers plodding desperate-faced. Men slavering and rolling their bare-teethed heads, slobbering and blowing, blasting brightness behind their eyeballs, supported by listless cripples.

French troops at Verdun showing the strain of battle.

Yet these are the ones who, officially, had stood up to battle conditions. Few of them would ever reach the shell-shock wards, because otherwise there would simply be no one left to man the trenches, Such fatigue was typical, such intense but wordless suffering was all part of a day's work.

On the whole the officers, because of their greater responsibilities, were less likely suddenly to break down in battle itself. Thus in the period August to October 1917 at the height of the Third Battle of Ypres, only one officer was admitted for every thirty-eight other ranks, whilst during the whole of the next twelve months the ratio was one to fourteen. When one also recalls that the proportion of officers to men was approximately one to thirty, this also indicates how much greater, in the long run, was the stress upon the line officer. As regards this greater resilience whilst actually under fire, perhaps an individual case history makes the point even more graphically, in this instance a mere NCO. He had been in France and Flanders from August 1914 to July 1915 without a break, yet appeared quite normal when his leave came up. He only collapsed, literally, on arriving at Victoria, and later examination found that this was because of his dread of being unable to face whatever increased responsibilities might await him on his return. Yet in his eleven months abroad he had been wounded twice, gassed twice and buried under a house without seeming to show any particular ill-effect.

Whatever the differences in the occurrence of shell-shock, officers certainly got better treatment. They had a greater chance of being sent to a Rest Station – many officers were sent to hotels in the South of France for up to a month and were given much more time to recuperate. From one sample of just over 8,000 cases, between March and December 1918, only six per cent of officers suffering from 'neurasthenia' were returned to duty, and sixty-six per cent sent back to base, whereas figures for other ranks are twenty-seven and thirty-six per cent. In another batch of shell-shock cases back at base, thirteen per cent of the officers were returned to duty and twenty-five per cent sent back home, The men were given shorter shrift: only eighteen per cent got back to Britain, whilst forty-eight per cent were returned to duty.

PART THREE

A Lighter Side?

9 Sustaining the Men in the Line

In theory, at least, all the armies in France and Flanders were well fed. Considerable research had been carried out into the human body's calorific requirements, and every attempt was made to draw up a balanced daily diet. The best-fed troops were the Americans who were allotted a daily ration worth 4,714 calories. Next came the French with 4,466 calories, though this figure was somewhat artificial in that it included 600 calories to be provided with a daily money allowance of 35 centimes, the value of which was steadily eroded. The British were supposed to consume 4,193 calories per day, and finally came the Germans with 4,038. For all the armies this allowance only applied to front-line troops. All maintained what was known as a Lines of Communication Ration that was between two and seven hundred calories less. The basic components of these rations were bread, meat and vegetables. The Americans, not surprisingly, had the best meat ration, with $1\frac{1}{4}$ lbs daily. The British received 1 lb and the French marginally less. The German allotment, at the beginning of the war, was only 12 ounces. Vegetables were of varying importance. The British were given over half a pound a day, the Germans over a pound. For the French there was no fixed allocation, whereas the Americans were expected to make do with $1\frac{1}{4}$ lbs potatoes. According to British dieticians, these rations were surplus to requirements. A man needed only 3,574 calories per day. But they charitably recognised that war makes extraordinary demands on the human body and thus:

> ...a certain degree of surplus consumption is absolutely essential. The soldier in training for the battlefield should carry on his own person reserves in the form of fat or other material. The only method by which these internal reserves can be formed is by giving a definite surplus of food for long periods before the strain begins.

But these allocations were extremely theoretical. Perhaps the requisite amount of food did leave England; the recorded total is 3,240,948 tons of it. But nothing like this quantity ever got to the troops actually at the front. Vast amounts of it were lost, pilfered or simply thrown away. This was particularly true for the troops in the front-line trenches. Both in quantity and quality their rations left much to be desired. One of the greatest problems was supplying the forward trenches with hot food. Until late 1915 this was not even attempted. Whilst they were in the trenches the men lived on bread, bully beef and biscuits. Eventually the authorities began to bring the company field-kitchens up as close as possible, and as soon as the food had been cooked it was carried up the communication trenches in dixies, petrol cans or old jam tins, usually carried in a straw-lined box. Even so, by the time the

Cooks in the field.

food actually arrived it was usually cold. Nor was there any official provision for reheating it, or for cooking in the trenches themselves. Fires were usually strictly forbidden, and the only method was the so-called Tommy Cooker, a pocket-sized solidified-alcohol stove which gave out a slow weak heat. Sometimes three or four men in a platoon would club together to buy a small primus stove and use it for brewing their tea and warming their joint rations. But these were not government issue and thus it was very difficult to obtain fresh supplies of fuel. Some men improvised their own cookers. A favourite device was to soak the pull-through rag for one's rifle in whale-oil and light it in an old cigarette tin. The flame usually lasted long enough to heat up a mess-tin of water.

During a battle there was very little chance of receiving hot food or, indeed, any food at all. Time and time again troops were continually cut off for days on end with only the food and water they had brought with them. Then they had to fall back on their emergency iron rations which could only be opened with an officer's permission. But few men would have voluntarily consumed them, except in the direst emergency, for in all the armies they were uniformly unappetising. Basically they consisted of a tin of bully beef, a few biscuits, a small sealed tin of tea and sugar, and a wedge of mouldy cheese. Of course these iron rations did not last long, and once they were gone there was nothing to do but sit tight and pray to be relieved. Sometimes particularly desperate measures were adopted. In September 1914 it proved impossible to get through to certain isolated French units and the cooks actually had to crawl as close as they could and throw food into the trenches. The lack of water could be particularly trying. On occasions men were reduced to drinking their own urine or boiling up the water lying at the bottom of a shell hole. This was extremely hazardous as the water was inevitably polluted by a rotting corpse or the vestiges of a gas cloud.

Not only did the men usually get less than the official ration, but that itself was eroded as the war went on. For the British the main reason for this was the impossibility of finding enough ships to transport it. In the winter of 1917-18 an official campaign was launched with the slogan 'Eat Less and Save Shipping'. It was an unfortunate choice of words; almost immediately the exhortation was changed to 'Eat Less and Save Shitting'. The situation for the French was much worse. In December 1915 their supply and distribution system almost completely broke down. A commission of enquiry found that of the 300,000 field-kitchens almost half were totally unserviceable. When at this time the Army propaganda section announced that every man at the front got two good meals a day, they were inundated with 200,000 enraged letters from the men in the trenches.

But it was the Germans who suffered most of all from shortages. They were very badly hit by the Allied blockade and as the war went on they found it impossible to maintain

The mid-day meal in the front line trenches.

their original ration assessments. In June 1916 the meat ration was cut from twelve to ten ounces, and in the following October a further four ounces were lopped off. In June 1916 it was officially laid down that there should be one meatless day per week, but by 1918 troops not actually in action were given meat on only nine days of each month. The daily bread ration was also cut in April 1917. And what food they did get by this stage was generally appalling. For a while the staple dish was pea-soup with a few lumps of fat and gristle. In the winter of 1916-17, known as the 'Turnip Winter', even this was a rarity. Standard delicacies were bread made of dried ground turnips and saw-dust. To add a little flavour, a paste was supplied, this time made of mashed turnip. The troops referred to it as 'Hindenburg fat'. Occasionally a kind of stew was provided, but the cooks were obliged to use horsemeat and the dried vegetables in it were predominantly nettles. It became a standard fatigue for soldiers in support to be sent out on a nettle-picking expedition. They soon came to refer to dried vegetables as 'barbed-wire entanglements'.

Indeed the quality of food given to all the armies was very poor. For the French the official definition of 'fresh' bread was anything that had been baked within the last eight days. By the time a loaf had left a British bakery in the base area, and travelled up to the men who were actually to eat it, it was inevitably quite stale. Nor was the meat much better. On the Western Front it was usually bully or pressed beef, what the French referred to as *singe* (monkey). Even when meat appeared in a stew, it was more fat than anything else. As the war went on the British began to rely heavily on tinned mixtures such as 'meat and vegetable', imortalised under the manufacturer's name as Maconochie. It consisted largely of sliced turnips and carrots and a deal of thin soup or gravy. As one soldier pointed out: 'Warmed in the tin, Maconochie was edible; cold it was a mankiller.' Another tinned favourite was pork and beans. The beans were haricot beans and the pork nothing more than fat, exactly what we today would call 'baked beans'. The Official History includes a rather plaintive comment on the troops understandable propensity to bolt the stuff down without chewing it: 'In some cases the full nutritive value...was not utilised as many men swallowed the beans without chewing them and they appeared unchanged in the faeces.' One can only assume that someone actually went round looking.

Army biscuit was described by Private Pressey of the Royal Artillery as being

> ...so hard that you had to put them on a firm surface and smash them with a stone or something. I've held one in my hand and hit the sharp corner of a brick wall and only hurt my hand...Sometimes we soaked the smashed fragments in water for several days. Then we would heat and drain, pour condensed milk over a dishful of the stuff and get it down.

Another method of serving the biscuits was to smash them into a pulp, add a few sultanas, and boil the mixture up in a sandbag. This would then be carried down to the trenches where each man would saw himself a piece off – sandbag and all. A private in the 5th Sherwood Foresters, R.B. Raisin, recalled his memories of a tour on Vimy Ridge in March 1916: 'Emergency biscuits were issued. We experimented with these by soaking and cooking...to form a sort of pudding. I revolt at the memory.'

Almost everything that the military authorities provided proved a disappointment. The British issued the troops with lots of jam, most of it made by a firm called Ticklers. The mixture soon became just as boring as everything else, for the only flavour supplied was plum and apple. Later equally doubtful mixtures, such as gooseberry or rhubarb, were added; at the same time the tins were replaced by cardboard cylinders. 'To the end an issue of strawberry or raspberry jam was an historic occasion.' Even the issue of sugar was made unnecessarily complicated. Captain G.B. Manwaring explained why in a letter to his sister: 'Why do they mix tea and sugar, I wonder? It's awfully annoying when one wants the sugar for other things – tea in one's coffee, on one's pancakes or apple tart, and I may tell you it's extraordinarily difficult to separate successfully – we do our best, but still seem full of tea.'

But such mixtures of tastes were the general rule. A field cooker only had two large vats, in which everything was prepared. Thus the tea usually had a strong flavour of meat and vegetables. Nor did the water help much. To purify it liberal quantities of chloride of lime were added which did little for the flavour. As Harold Chapin wrote,

My chief objection is the *Thé-à*-la-chloride-of-lime...In theory it sterilises the water and then settles, leaving no

perceptible flavour. In practice, it may sterilise the water all right, but it resolutely declines to altogether settle.

The water was made worse by being carried round in old petrol cans. Finally, of course, it was impossible to adequately clean one's personal canteen. For the British this was simply an almost oval container with a lid. Almost everything went into the lower section, from stew and soup to rice, tea and porridge. After a while the identification of the contents was done by sight alone.

Of course, the men did not have to subsist entirely on Army rations. They could buy a few extras with their pay at the battalion canteen or one of the YMCA or Red Cross huts back

British troops refilling their dixies just behind the front line.

at the camp. Alternatively they could get a meal at one of the *estaminets* behind the lines. However the choice was invariably limited to omelettes or fried egg and chips, so much so that the La Bassée sector was known as the 'Egg and Chip Front'. There were also food parcels from home, though the officers, not surprisingly, fared much better in this respect. Most of them received something from England regularly and in many companies there was a constant flow of hampers from Harrods or Fortnum and Mason's. Officers' servants also procured extra food for them and cooked it. Typical meals, even in the trenches, would include fresh meat, fish, fresh vegetables, salad, potted meats, cake, tinned fruit, cheese, dates or chocolate.

All ranks however had one thing in common, and this was

that all food was freely shared. To a large extent this was simply a reflection of the remarkable sense of comradeship that existed in the trenches. However, there were also much more mundane reasons. We have already seen how loaded down the troops were, and it should not be surprising that they were loathe to burden themselves with perishable items of food. Harold Chapin carefully explained the point in a letter to his wife:

> Every blessed thing we possess has to be carried with us on our backs. Some of the fellows get supplies of *sugar* sent to them – a mere waste of postage – others six pairs of sox! If they are wise they give them away. Food can always be eaten, if not by me personally by a small party convened by me, each member of which will assuredly invite me to his party when his box arrived – see?

The other basic necessity issued to the troops was drink. The rum ration was introduced in late 1914 as a means of counteracting the worst effects of the climate. It arrived at the front in one-gallon earthenware jugs, one jug for every sixty-four men. They had been laid down at Deptford for use in the Boer War and were marked with the letters SRD – Services Rum Diluted – translated in the trenches as 'Soon Runs Dry'. By 1918 each division on the British front was consuming 300 gallons per week, an average of one-third of a pint of rum per man per week, hardly enough to create an army of drunkards. The only men suspected of regularly getting more than their share were the orderlies who assisted the officer in charge of doling it out. It was generally claimed that they kept their thumb in the measuring dipper, thus ensuring a large last portion. Even when an officer was not present, there were none of the bacchanalian consequences that the authorities seem to have expected. In 1916 an officer of the King's Own Yorkshire Light Infantry wrote to *The Times* relating how he had recently been obliged to send the rum jar round without his being present. He had attached a note to it saying: 'Think of the other fellow and pass it on.' When it reached the last man it was still half-full. The French and German spirit ration was similar though theirs was a kind of rough brandy, rather than rum. The Germans referred to theirs as '98 per cent' and were officially allowed 0.17 of a pint each day. The French equivalent was known as *gnôle*, described by one infantryman as a 'cross between methylated spirits and paregoric elixir'. The French and Germans also had an official wine ration, in each case just less than a pint a day. The French called it *le pinard* and most men had some of the rough red wine in their canteens at all times. An American Executive Order, on the other hand, forbade the supplying of alcohol to the troops.

But the men were not entirely dependent upon the official allowances.* When resting there was some opportunity to visit one of the thousands of little *estaminets*. Anyone in Flanders could set up shop, and if after three months it had not been closed down the owner had a permanent right to operate. They were usually run by an old woman – a man was almost unheard of – assisted by various of her daughters and nieces. They sold rough spirits, wine and watery beer. The latter was so poor that both the British and Germans were obliged to import their own, and in 1918 the Quartermaster-General went into the brewing business, importing just the malt and hops rather than barrels of beer. When the French were resting they stuck almost exclusively to wine, of which there never seemed to be any shortage, even in the trenches.

The authorities were always afraid that drunkenness would become an escape from the chronic ghastliness of life on the Western Front. In fact in none of the armies does it seem to have been a serious problem in the line; the officers were much too observant for this. There were occasional exceptions of course. Usually it was a case of someone getting hold of the rum jar, often the men assigned to bring it up from the stores. Carrington tells of a ration party in 1917, who

> had got lost…had wandered all night and finally decided that the company was annihilated. Not without good sense they decided not to starve. They did their best with a whole company's rations, but a whole company's rum defeated them. Hither they had wandered very happy and very sleepy, but rather inclined to sing themselves to sleep.

It was decided that no further action should be taken on the matter. Another soldier, that same year, was less fortunate. He managed to get hold of the rum jar just before an attack and started kicking up a row. An officer shouted to someone to keep him quiet and later found his body, where he had been bayoneted.

Occasionally there were instances of more general drunkenness, during an advance or retreat, when men came across whole stocks of abandoned drink. The battalion diary of the 6th Durham Light Infantry refers obliquely to such an incident in late 1915. A cache of absinthe and brandy was discovered in a cellar in Houplines and 'there was a certain amount of trouble which was soon checked by Battalion and Company Sergeant-Majors'. During the aftermath of the

---

*This was just as well as some units were 'dry'. General Pinney, of the 33rd Division, a teetotaller, forbade the issue of rum except in emergencies and General Haldane forbade it throughout the dreaded 6th Corps. The Canadian 11th Brigade were always known as the 'Pea-soupers' because their commander had, temporarily, insisted on replacing the rum rations with an issue of pea-soup.

Battle of Arras in May 1917 an Australian soldier spoke of overtaking 'stragglers, some of them carrying about as much rum as they could hold.' A British machine gun officer told an almost incredible story of an incident during the retreat of March 1918. He and his adjutant 'discovered in the Belle Croix *estaminet*...a crowd of stragglers, fighting drunk. We routed them out, and with a machine gun trained on them, sent them towards the enemy. They perished to a man.' Despite these incidents drink was not a serious problem in the British Army. Between 1914 and March 1920 in all theatres of the war, General, District and Field General Court Martial tried 169,104 cases of all kinds. Of these only 35,313 were for drunkenness, slightly more than twenty per cent of the total and a minute proportion of the total number of troops who fought in these theatres.

British and French troops sharing 'le Pinard'.

The problem was more serious in the French and German armies. Though they had little access to dangerous quantities of drink whilst actually in the line, it figured prominently in their lives whilst resting or in reserve. Rudolph Binding noted that whereas in 1914 and early 1915 his corps had been sending home $1\frac{1}{2}$ million marks every month, the new availability of German wine and beer in the rear areas had suddenly cut that figure by half. In the French rear areas drunkenness was still more of a problem. General Pétain gave it as one of the causes of the mutinies of 1917:

> The example comes from the messes of the lieutenants where they have taken up the habit of drinking to excess. The NCOs naturally follow this same error. The result is that, among the men, drink has become so important that they hesitate to begin a march without filling their canteens with wine.

A French officer recalled the men he had known who had succumbed to the joint pressure of the strain of the trenches and the utter boredom of the rest periods: 'How many of them I knew, those poor sods, sober before 1914, who, because of hunger and thirst in the midst of the machine guns, have lost their bearings as they tried to reach out to forgetfulness from the bottom of their flask of *pinard* or their issue of *gnôle*.' When the mutinies had been suppressed, Pétain issued orders that greatly restricted the flow of wine into the Army Zones, both to the troops and to the civilians who might want to resell it. He also completely prohibited the sale of wine in rest camps on the day before the troops were to leave for the front.

But drunkenness had its most significant strategic effect during the great German offensive of 1918. Whilst it is going too far to suggest that it tipped the balance, it is clear from the official accounts that in many instances the push forward was seriously delayed by units who could not tear themselves away from the vast dumps of alcohol that fell into their hands.

> At Soissons the desire for such loot brought the forfeit of opportunity. At Fismes there were 'drunken soldiers lying all over the road'. At Jonchery 'battalions stopped in the face of the slightest opposition and it was difficult to get them together again. Progress was very slow although there was no actual fighting. At the villages lamentable disorders took place. The officers could no longer keep control…a sorry picture of much drunkenness.'

An even more important psychological comfort than either food or drink was communication with home, the sending and receiving of letters from families and friends. Here was an essential link with pre-war reality, a glimpse of sanity.

Whether in the trenches or resting all soldiers spent a good deal of their time writing letters or reading and rereading even the most banal communications from home. Vast quantities of mail went between France and Britain every day. In 1914 the Postal Section of the Royal Engineers had a staff of 250 men. By 1918 the newly formed Army Postal Service had 4,000 soldiers working for it. Twelve and a half million letters were sent out to all fronts each week, and almost every one elicited a reply. The bulk of the parcel post was equally gigantic and the parcel section of the APS occupied a five-acre wooden building in Regents Park. Officers, in particular, were quite accustomed to receiving regularly large hampers from home, or the major department stores, as well as whole cases of spirits and wine. One officer, Philip Gosse sent off to Harrods for two mole-traps and received them, at the front, within a week. On the whole the mail arrived remarkably quickly. A

Christmas post on the Western Front.

letter usually took no more than two or three days and very few letters failed to reach their destination. Even during the chaotic retreat of March 1918 only three bags of mail were lost. The armies fully realised the immense importance of the post and every effort was made to get it to the men as soon as possible. They did not have to wait until they were in reserve or resting to receive a backlog of letters, but received them daily, even when in the front line. A company's sack of letters and parcels was brought up with the ration party. As long as the food and drink could get through so did the mail. This was the high spot of the daily grind as parcels were opened and shared out, letters read and often passed to the few unfortunates who had received no mail.

Many of the men at the front were only technically literate and had no experience of translating their feelings into words. So the average letter from the front was at best a rather

Writing home from Messines. The letters usually reached home in two or three days.

prosaic document. But there was another reason for this in that the men were always at pains to conceal the reality of what was happening from their loved ones back home. French soldiers were particularly sensitive on this point. One wrote:

> In these pathetic post-cards, bloodied and dirty, the *poilus* had the supreme nobility of spirit to keep on lying and say: 'resting for a long time', 'nothing is happening', 'looking forward to seeing you soon'.

At times this sense of isolation from the world outside the trenches became almost a contempt for those who had not experienced the horrors of trench warfare: 'For the benefit of those in the rear we edited a correspondence full of convenient lies, lies about how well things were going. We described *their* war to them, which satisfied them and we kept ours a secret.' There was also the problem of censorship. All letters had to be read by the orderly officer of the day, although in the British Army it was possible to obtain a green envelope, the contents of which could not be read. This however, was a rare privilege. Many officers could not, in fact, bring themselves to read other men's letters, but the knowledge that they might placed a severe restriction upon a soldier's freedom of expression.

The average letter or post-card from France was a very trite, stereotyped document. One British officer, Lieutenant A.G. Heath of the 6th Royal West Kents, once drafted what was meant as a typical letter from one of his privates and his effort reveals the enormous disparity between what men were going through and what they were able, or willing to communicate:

> Just a few loving lines in answer to your kind and loving letter and Thanking you for the two beautiful parcels which has come in very handy, the cake was quite unbroken and me and my mates enjoyed it very much in the trenches. Dear Mrs. we have been six days and nights under fire, but the Germans will never advance near they are afraid of our rifle fire...We are back now for a bit of a rest and we can do with it too but every night we dig trenches under fire. We shall go into the trenches again soon and after that we come on leave so that I shall see you and the two dear Babies again. Ho what joyful times we shall have when this is all over. We are fed up with it but we keep smiling. Dear Mrs. I will close for the censor will not let us say anything. Hoping you are in the Pink as it leaves me...

Post-cards were much more common than letters, and the following might be taken as typical of the many millions that passed to and fro. It is dated 24 July 1915 from 'BEF France', 'Just a few lines hoping you and Sid and family are getting on alright as it leaves me the same at present. Thanks for

Behind the lines: German troops reading of their latest victory.

cigarettes they come in very handy. I will send you a post-card later. I am sending George one. Yours affectionately Brother Jim.' But the very use of such trite clichés was an attempt to reduce the war to the same predictable and rather trivial routine that governed ordinary life back home. Banality meant a stability of sorts. One lieutenant, R.E. Vernède, told of a boy in his platoon who every day wrote exactly the same letter to his family, three pages of 'in the pink', 'not arf' and 'keep merry and bright', etc. 'It goes on like that for three pages, absolutely fixed; and if he has to say anything definite, like acknowledging a parcel, he has to put in a separate letter – not to interfere with the sacred order of things.'

10 Rest and Leave

O, O, O it's a lovely War!
What do we want with eggs and ham
When we have plum and apple jam?
Form fours, right turn,
How shall we spend the money we earn?
O, O, O it's a lovely War!

'Tommies' arriving home at Mud Terrace, billets just behind the line.

Out of the line the soldiers had some chance of rest and relaxation. In billets, just behind the line, this was very limited because one might be expected to move off again at any time. Even so, it was a pleasant contrast with the filth and squalor of the trenches proper and at least the soldiers had a roof over their heads. Officers usually had the best accommodation, as the rates paid to civilians for the use of billets show. In 1914, a lieutenant-general was worth five francs, a captain one franc and a private a mere 21 centimes – only 5 centimes if there was no straw available. But as the war progressed proper billets became increasingly scarce as property was pounded to rubble. Artificial accommodation became more and more common. At first tents were used, then wooden huts, though these were soon superseded by the familiar Canadian Nissen hut. By mid-1917, 50,000 of them had been brought across to France.

But even in rest camps proper, near or in the Base Areas the men were not allowed to lounge around and please themselves. Charles Carrington summed up the Army's conception of 'rest' when he said 'In the Great War [it] meant stiff military training all the morning and games in the afternoon.' General Jack's timetable for a typical day of divisional rest shows clearly how even the officers had little time to themselves. Reveille was at 6 a.m. followed by the roll-call at 7. The men then washed and cleaned their arms and equipment before breakfast at 8. From 9 a.m. until noon everyone was occupied with inspections of arms equipment and quarters followed by a lengthy drill session. Dinner followed and then organised games until 4 p.m. The men not on guard duty were then free to amuse themselvs until lights out at 9.30. The essence of the system was the Army's fear of leaving men to their own devices. To allow soldiers too much opportunity to act and think as individuals, it was felt, might seriously undermine their automatic acceptance of army discipline. Even before a battalion left the trenches it had to submit a detailed programme of training activities to be undertaken during the rest period. The sport, too, was designed to foster military cohesion. Much of it consisted of competitions, from platoon level right up to inter-divisional sports, usually focusing upon some aspect of military life such as shooting or riding. Team games were encouraged – football for the men and rugby and cricket for the officers. Football became quite a mania from 1917 onwards. As a member of the 39th Field Ambulance wrote: 'Our football was ubiquitous and no part of the Quartermaster's Stores was guarded so jealously and packed so securely when we were on the march as the leather sphere which played so large a part in the life of the men when at rest.'

Even the men's evenings were often organised for them with divisional concerts. Most divisions could find within their

Boxing at No. 15 Convalescent Depot, Trouville.

numbers a certain number of men who had had some experience of entertaining their fellows, and two or three of these were usually held back at headquarters to form the nucleus of a concert party, such as 'The Follies' of the 4th Division, 'The Lads' of the 42nd Division or 'The Mountebanks' of the 132nd Field Ambulance. Other well-known names were 'The Bow Bells', 'The Jocks', 'The Pipsqueaks' 'The Whizz Bangs', 'The Brass Hats' and 'The Verey Lights'. Most divisions provided concerts on at least two days a week, and they were also organised, on a much more impromptu basis, at battalion and brigade level. The latter tended to be more popular with the troops as the material was more adapted to their tastes. One trench newspaper, the *Sub Rosa*, the organ of the West Lancashire Division, spoke of this in describing two distinct types of revue,

the Sophisticated, composed of pre-war professionals [whose] jokes generally require an intimate knowledge of Town to appreciate...[and] the Primitive, composed of amateurs, nearer to and better understood [sic] of their audience. Their jests are possily heavier, but certainly more direct, and they are much more obviously in love with their work of lightening the strain on their fellow men.

'The Duds' 17th Divisional Concert party.

Not least because the entertainers themselves had had experience of that strain and might expect to endure it again after this brief interval.

The programme was usually a mixture of songs and sketches. 'The Mountebanks' for example offered the following songs – 'There's a Land', 'Just Another One', 'Nita Gitana', 'Proud I am', 'Come Under My Umbrella', 'I Wanted to Go Back', 'Carmena' and 'For Me And My Girl' – interspersed with a couple of sketches and a monologue. This was followed by an interval and then one long sketch involving the whole company. In 1916 the 6th Infantry Reinforcements (NZEF) arranged a concert of their own. It began with a rendering on violin of Paderewski's Valse de Concert. Then the Colonel stepped forward to sing 'Ching Chong Chinaman', after which the whole company sang 'The Village Pump', with the audience joining in the rousing chorus. Someone then gave a recital of the immortal monologue 'Gunga Din' and there followed a series of sketches ranging from broad to obscene. At other concerts, between each 'turn' the audience often roared out a chorus:

Jolly good song,
Jolly well sung.

If you can think of a better you're welcome to try,
But don't forget the singer is dry;
Give the poor bugger some beer.

Sometimes an effort was made to offer a more coherent entertainment. An army doctor described one concert that he attended in 1917 which seems to have been the product of a rather sardonic sense of humour:

During our last tour out I went to a Show. It is a kind of Divisional Follies, but none the less good for that. A sort of Panto, all done by men who have been over the Top, or at least done front line work...The plot is laid in 1967, and is really awfully clever. War still progressing, and the men's grandsons were rolling up. Leave only granted once in twenty-one years.

Other sorts of organised entertainment were offered. Famous names from London came to the rear areas to sing or present plays. Harry Lauder tells the story of 'one of our really great serious actors' who came over to entertain the troops in hospital. Unfortunately he insisted on giving a spirited recital of Longfellow's 'Wreck of the Hesperus'. After a few stanzas a voice suddenly piped up, 'To cover men', and the rest of the recital was to rows of heaped bedclothes, not a head being visible. Lauder himself went to France and seems to have made every effort to get as near to the front as possible, his only son having been killed there in December 1916. He travelled around in a motor-car with a vicar, a Member of Parliament, an accompanist and a small portable piano that had been specially made for him. The whole entourage came to be known to the troops as The Reverend Harry Lauder MP Show.

Regimental bands were also very popular. At first the War Office would not allow them anywhere near the front, but by mid-1915 they were a feature of every rest camp, giving concerts at all times of the day, particularly a meal-times. At one stage a battalion's stretcher-bearers were supposed to be taken from the musicians, but as the war progressed the link became purely nominal, the bandsmen being carefully protected well away from the front. Cinemas were also beginning to be popular, and some units provided a screen of their own. The cinema at 3rd Division Headquarters had a special gallery for officers in which they could take tea and cakes as they watched the film. Charlie Chaplin, who made his first films in 1914, was the particular sensation. For music the ordinary soldiers were dependent on mouth-organs, penny-whistles, combs and paper, but many officers had their own gramophones which were sometimes taken into the trenches, playing anything from the Charlie Chaplin Walk to Schubert and Elgar.

Reading the news in the
trenches — 1000 yards
from the German lines.

Reading was not a very popular occupation. The
rank-and-file were barely literate, and for most of them
reading a novel would have been more of a chore than a
relaxation. At first newspapers were avidly read because they
at least should have been offering hard information with a
specific bearing on the soldiers' situation. But since war-time
censorship was so strict that newspaper reports were at best
evasive and at worst crude distortions, the troops swiftly
learned to regard any newspaper report with little more than
amused contempt. The Army did in fact provide a War
Library, and various societies were set up in England to
provide reading matter for the troops, but these had very little
effect. Philip Gosse remembered that his mother kept him

> ...well supplied with books...When I had read these they
> were passed on to others...who liked reading something
> other than occasional newspapers or cheap magazines,

which was all that ever came their way...I heard, after the War, that some philanthropic people in England formed a committee to collect books and send them out to the men in the trenches, but certainly none of the books ever got to our division.

But the ordinary soldier, or even officer, who wanted something substantial to read was the exception. Stephen Graham of the Scots Guards wrote of the reading habits of the majority of the soldiers: 'What the men do read is Florence Warden and Charles Garvice, and books with such titles as *The Temptress, Red Rube's Revenge, The Lost Diamonds* – gaudy adventure stories which can be torn for cigarette lights later on. All prefer, however, to look at the pictures rather than read.'

Not all the amenities and amusements available to the soldiers were free. For other things they had to fork out from their own pay, which for all armies, was uniformly meagre. A British private received a shilling per day, although there were a few stoppages taken out of this sum every week. A French ranker was given 2½d. per day. In March 1917 the French made an attempt to distinguish between veterans and others. A decree of that month gave special rates of pay to all those with two years service over the legal minimum. There was also to be a special gratuity for all those who had been in battle. The German private of 1914 received the pathetic sum of 1¾d. per day. There were variations within the Imperial Forces. Canadian soldiers got $1 per week and the New Zealanders were the best paid of all. Even the situation within the British Army was not completely uniform. Cavalrymen received more than infantrymen and the Guards cavalry even more. Specialised troops fared better as well. Artillerymen were on a slightly higher scale and a private in the Army Ordnance Corps got six shillings per day.

In all armies officers were much better paid, and on active service one encountered the unique situation of many young officers managing to survive on their own pay, an impossible task in time of peace. At the beginning of the war, a British subaltern received 5s. 3d. per day, raised in 1915 to 7s. 6d. This was a basic rate on top of which there was a daily field allowance of 2s. 6d., an equivalent lodgings allowance and a mess allowance of 9d. to drink the King's health. By 1918 an English lieutenant was getting 19s. 6d. per day. The Germans were not so fortunate. The stringent situation at home forced the government to reduce the rate for officers in October 1916, though the new scales only applied to those promoted after that date.

Incredibly, many men did manage to save some of their pay and send it back home. One indication is the number of postal orders sold in France, which had an average weekly value of

British troops attend a lecture at the ubiquitous YMCA hut.

£56,000. One way of spending the money was on various little luxuries that could be obtained in camp. By late 1915 all rest camps were equipped with at least one small shop run by the YMCA or the Red Cross. Here one could buy cigarettes, post-cards, basic groceries, razor-blades and such-like. The YMCA hut was a particularly important focus of the camp. They were usually quite large, forty to eighty feet long, and as well as the shop they provided a lunch counter and a large hall equipped with tables and chairs in the daytime, for reading and writing letters, and in the evening offered the usual venue for a lecture or a concert. Also, from February 1915 each battalion provided its own canteen. At first this had been regarded as a needless luxury. In August of the previous year Kitchener had dismissed the idea, pointing out that 'This war is not going to be a picnic'. In theory the battalion provided both a 'dry' and a 'wet' canteen where alcohol could be brought, but many commanders did not bother with the latter.

A large percentage of the men's pay, therefore, was spent in the local *estaminets*. For the rest there were two main outlets – gambling and whoring. For many men, on all sides, gambling became quite an obsession, the chance of multiplying one's pay being about the only variation in a life of deadeningly predictable monotony. Card games were most popular, largely because a pack was easily carried. In every platoon there would be at least man with a battered and greasy deck of cards, always looking for an opportunity, no matter how fleeting, to play a few hands. T.S. Hope, a private in a Scottish regiment, marvelled at their stamina: 'What puzzles me is just how little sleep these card players can exist on. In support, reserve or back in billets, always the same little parties. They play cards and gamble whenever they have a minute off duty, snatching an occasional hour of sleep at odd times, mostly when they are broke.' The most popular card games were

A cavalry division rest their horses at a French village.

Brag and Bank or Banker, a type of *vingt-et-un*. Card games were also the most common form of gambling in the French Army where different games were played according to the regions the troops came from. The most frequently played were *mariage*, *piquet* and *piquet-voleur*, and *manille* or *manoche* as it was known, the equivalent of today's *belote*. But these were the games of the privates and non-commissioned officers.

It is in card-playing pehaps, that rank produced the most marked differences...many officers played poker. But it was above all bridge that was the rage in the officers' mess; it was in its early stages: a modified form of whist, with bids, with none of the subtleties of contract-bridge...It was played on rest, but also in the line when in a quiet sector and the officers could muster a four.

For the Germans, too, gambling was an important pastime. Here the most popular card games were *Skat* and *Doppelkopf*, as well as the old army gambling game, *Mauschelm*, and a

A skittle alley in the German reserve trenches.

rather bizarre game called *Wattepusten*, which is based upon the players' ability to blow little tufts of cotton-wool around. For the Americans dice or 'craps' was the big favourite. It had always been associated with the army and is supposed to have been invented by the all-Negro regiments in the 1890s. Gambling was probably more prevalent in the US Army than any other and very large sums of money regularly changed hands. One observer was driven to complain: 'If [gambling] is as widespread as these young men admit, I'm not sure but that wine and women are less serious evils.'

Out of the line the most popular games of chance in the British Army were not card games but House and Crown and Anchor. House – the predecessor of bingo – was the only gambling game officially allowed by the authorities. Discs and cards, marked with a variety of numbers, were used and one filled in the card as the appropriate numbers were pulled out of a bag. The first to complete his card – to get a 'Full House' – was the winner. The game was run by a banker who offered his cards with such ritual cries as

Housey, Housey, who'll have a card?
You come here in wheelbarrows
And go away in motor-cars.

Crown and Anchor involved a dice and a piece of cloth marked with six symbols: a crown, an anchor, a club, a heart, a spade and a diamond. These were usually referred to as the Major, the Mud-hook, the Shamrock, the Jam-tart, the Curse and the Kinkie. The stake was put on one symbol and if it came up when the dice was thrown the banker paid out. Choosing the right symbol was a compulsive thing for many soldiers. As Stephen Graham wrote:

The experience of a soldier's life in escaping death and wounds impresses him with the idea of a lucky chance. War breeds gambling as a natural and inevitable fruit.

Of course, in the long run only the banker won. The odds were very much in his favour and many men at the front have related seeing a banker cleaning up a thousand francs in one or two days. Like crap dealers and some bingo callers today a Crown and Anchor banker would keep up an extraordinary stream of patter to encourage the punters: 'Here we are again. The Sweaty Socks! Cox and Co.; the Army bankers, badly bent but never broken, safe as the Bank of England, undefeated because they never fought; the rough and tough, the old and bold! Where you lay, we pay. If you don't speculate, you can't accumulate.'

When British troops left for France they were all given a message from Lord Kitchener which they had to stick in their

Active Service Paybooks. Amongst other things the letter urged the troops to be on their guard against certain temptations:

> Your duty cannot be done unless your health is sound, so keep constantly on your guard against any excesses. In this new experience you may find temptations both in wine and women. You must entirely resist both temptations and while treating women with perfect courtesy, you should avoid any intimacy.

This message was not much heeded. Sexual deprivation does not seem to have been a very pressing problem for much of the time, but when men were resting or on leave the natural urges tended to reassert themselves. Some men felt them more keenly than others. An American soldier wrote to his wife 'Take a long look at the floor, Martha, because when I get home you aren't going to see anything but the ceiling for a long, long time.' Charles Carrington wrote: 'The popular line the Army followed, at every grade, was the pursuit of sex, on the rare days when opportunity offered. A compensation was found for sex-starvation in the recourse to bawdy jokes and rhymes, of which there was a never-failing supply.

One indication of sexual activity by the troops was the very high incidence of venereal disease which afflicted twice as many victims as any other disease in the trenches. Between 1914 and 1918, 153,531 cases of venereal disease are recorded. Yet, the researches of Colonel Asburn of the US Army, and Colonel Harrison, of the British, indicated 'that the all-round risk of infection from illicit sexual intercourse without precautions is about three per cent.' Clearly, then, there was a great deal of 'illicit sexual intercourse' going on. The French forces suffered over one million cases of venereal disease, one fifth of them involving syphilis. The Americans waged a particularly intensive campaign against it and by the end of the war they had cut the rate to eleven cases per thousand men, well below that of any other army.

Judging from the VD rates, the Dominion troops seem to have been particularly active. In 1916, for example, the British Army in the UK had a VD rate of 36.7 cases per thousand men, whilst the Canadian had 209.4 per thousand. The Australians in 1917 suffered a 'casualty' rate of eighty-five men per thousand, against a more modest British total of thirty-two, even though the Australians and New Zealanders issued their men with individual disinfection kits long before the British. When the British did begin to favour such measures, they placed the bottles of potassium permanganate lotion and tubes of calomel cream in the latrines, where anyone needing treatment was forced to reveal it to his fellows. Not until November 1918 did the British give soldiers individual supplies and they were never as generous as the New Zealanders, who provided six prophylactic tubes every time they went on leave. Quite a proportion of the VD infections in France were brought back from England but the greater proportion originated in France itself. All the armies permitted the troops to visit brothels, known as *maisons de tolérance* in the large cities. These were regularly inspected by the authorities. The Germans, for example, visited each one twice a week and every effort was made to weed out infected women. As usual a distinction was made between officers and men. In the British forces the men visited those establishments sporting the traditional red lamp, but for the former a more sober blue was the practice. There is some dispute as to how well patronised these places were. Robert Graves spoke of a brothel in Calais outside which he

...had seen a queue of a hundred and fifty men waiting outside the door, each to have his short turn with one of the three women in the house…Each woman served nearly a battalion of men every week for as long as she lasted. According to the assistant provost marshal three weeks was the usual limit: 'After which she retired on her earnings, pale but proud.'

T.S. Hope, on the other hand, wrote in his diary after a visit to Calais that if the men could 'capture a little pleasure of forgetfulness…who can blame them? Life is so very uncertain out here. Even so, I have not yet seen those mythical queues lined up outside a red lamp.' The official researches would also seem to indicate that long queues were the exception. Some military busybody actually counted the number of men patronising the brothels in a certain street in Le Havre. Over a twelve-month period it was visited by 171,000 men. Assuming even only six brothels on the street, this could mean that no more than 80 men visited each one every day.

The brothels were of uniform seediness. Any glimmerings of emotion or tenderness that might have accompanied the purely physical urge were swiftly dispelled. One description will suffice:

> He had entered the place at 1600 hours; his turn came up just before 1730. That old woman led him upstairs. She wore a leather pouch like a tramdriver. It jingled with money. Beyond the open door he saw a fattish half-undressed woman. He could not look at her after the first glance. She had thick ankles and legs in coarse black stockings. The room smelt musty…He tried to overcome his reluctance, increased by the sight of spittle on the floor.

The official attitude towards the men's sexual habits revealed a curious ambivalence. On the one hand, and this is perhaps surprising given the official attitudes of the time, they fully believed that men must find some sexual outlet to avoid physical or mental harm. Stephen Graham was quite emphatic on this point:

> Sexual intercourse was regarded as a physical necessity for the men. Besides being the medical point of view, it became the official army point of view as well, and we were often told in lectures that it was natural, and all we had to do was to use the safeguards and preventatives which were at our disposal to save us from disease.

Even so, the Army came down severely on those who actually contracted venereal disease. They were given hospital treatment – a special base hospital, number 9, was set aside for the purpose – but were clearly given to understand that they were to blame. For one thing, stoppages were made from

A drum head service.

a soldier's pay. Officers had to pay 2s. 6d. for every day they spent in hospital, the men 7d. Officers also lost their 2s. 6d. field allowance and any man receiving some sort of extra proficiency bonus immediately had this docked. Stoppages were normal for *any* illness not contracted through active service – but as every other illness except alcoholism was treated as so contracted, it seems fair to regard army policy as a form of penal sanction. On top of this, from 27 January 1917 anyone who contracted VD became ineligible, for twelve months, for any leave. In April 1918 the British made their policy a little less hypocritical by placing the *maisons de tolérance* out of bounds to all troops, though this was almost entirely in deference to religious pressure from the home front.

Official provision was also made for the spiritual welfare of the troops. In the British Army three chaplains were attached to each division, mostly Anglicans though with a fair sprinkling of Catholics, particularly in the Irish and Scottish units. In the German Army only one chaplain was allowed per division. The French official provision was equally low, but in actual fact a great many clergymen served as ordinary soldiers, partly out of choice and partly because most exemptions from military service had been suppressed in 1914.

The Catholic faith was much more appealing to the troops, since Mass, confession, and the last rites were all impressive ceremonies with the assurance of formality. For men who might meet death at any moment, such specific reassurances were a great psychological boon. Guy Chapman brought out this contrast between Catholic and Anglican practices: 'Already there was a growing dislike of these latter...The Church of Rome sent a man into action mentally and spiritually cleaned. The Church of England could only offer you a cigarette.'

There was a remarkable unanimity about the ineffective role of the Anglican establishment in the war. Indeed many ordinary chaplains, who officially were not allowed to go further forward than Brigade HQ themselves felt frustrated by the policies of their superiors. The contrast with Catholic padres is brought out by Robert Graves:

> For Anglican regimental chaplains we had little respect...[They were] under orders to avoid getting mixed up with the fighting and stay behind with the transport. Soldiers could hardly respect a chaplain who obeyed these orders, and yet not one in fifty seemed sorry to obey them...The colonel in one battalion I served with got rid of four new Anglican chaplains in four months; finally he applied for a Roman Catholic, alleging a change of faith in the men under his command. For Roman Catholic chaplains were not only permitted to visit posts of danger, but definitely enjoyed to be wherever fighting was, so that they could give extreme unction to the dying. And we never heard of one who failed to do all that was expected of him and more.

The private soldiers held just the same opinion simply because the Catholics proved themselves more courageous, more overtly concerned with their charges. Private Gilbert Hall of the 13th Yorkshire and Lancashire

> ...commented that the Roman Catholic padres were always very much in evidence in the front line, but some of the Anglican padres were never to be seen. This reflected on the congregations they were able to gather. If a padre had 'proved himself' by exposing himself to the same dangers as his 'parishioners' then the men would always give him a hearing.

For most men God remained in the background. One story told in France makes the point succinctly. A clergyman somehow finds himself caught up in a carriage of men on their way back to France. He cheerfully asks them 'So you are going to fight God's war?' There is no reply. He repeats his question even more ecstatically. Still there is no response. 'Don't you believe in God's war?' he demands. A soldier looks at him wearily, 'Sir, hadn't you better keep your poor Friend out of this bloody mess?'

The final official effort to make mens' lives bearable was leave. In all armies it lasted about ten days, including the journey home and back, and in all armies it was fairly infrequent. In the French Army it was not even put on a regular basis until August 1915 when the commanders finally realised that the war might drag on for months and even years. Then every man was supposed to go on leave once every four months but, because all leave could be cancelled if an offensive was imminent, few men got leave anything like as regularly as this. In the British Army officers generally fared better than the men and could expect to return home once every six to eight months whilst the soldiers were very lucky to make it once a year. Frank Hawkins of the 2nd Queen Victoria Rifles left for France in November 1914 and did not receive his first leave until the following November. Gilbert Hall arrived in France in December 1915 and did not return home until April 1917. In February 1917 there were many reports of men who had not had leave for sixteen to eighteen months whilst, at about the same time, Charles Carrington knew of men in his battalion who had not been home for twenty. The situation did not improve until the second half of 1918 when men could reliably expect to be granted leave after six months in France.

Clearly, then, official and unofficial efforts to give the men some sort of relaxation were not very adequate. The British methods apply equally to the Germans who had just the same 'light' reliefs of drink, sex, concerts and gambling. For the French, not even this much was provided. In their rest periods

'Back to Blighty' — boarding the leave boat.

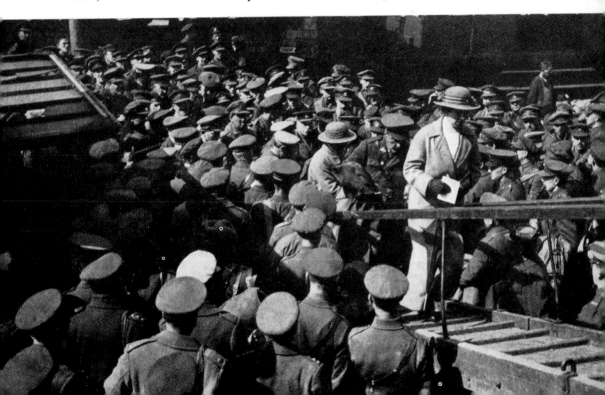

they were left entirely to their own devices. In theory this might sound attractive, bu the reality was quite different. Most of the rest areas were already occupied by rear echelon formations who had already monopolised the best accommodation and resented the intrusion of the front-line troops. The men often had to pay local peasants to find any accommodation at all, and even in the Permanent Zones of Rest there was hardly any provision of kitchens, showers or latrines. Until Pétain's reforms of 1917, men often had to sleep two to a bed. Prices were very high and the civilians made every effort to part the soldiers from their money as quickly as possible. Henri Barbusse related a typical conversation with a whining, old peasant woman at a village in which he was billeted: 'You see the military authorities forces them that's got wine to sell it at fifteen sous! Fifteen sous! The misery of this cursed war! One loses at it, at fifteen sous, sir. So I don't sell any wine.'

It is hardly surprising, therefore, that for French troops a period in billets or at rest could be nothing but a massive anti-climax. Jacques Meyer remembered the utter boredom that could soon set in:

What distractions were there? The same strolls that led the same men to the same places at the same times. You waited for the postman who would not have any letters for you. What monotony, what an empty existence. What a temptation to idleness, too, for the great knack was to avoid exercises and fatigues. The great problem was that of killing time. One felt only dreary sluggishness.

And yet, when all this is said, there were moments of intense pleasure to be had, brief interludes of a refined sense of peace, of liberation that could never be attained in a more stable environment. Many soldiers have spoken of this duality of extremes. Daniel Mornet wrote of his days at Verdun:

After letters from our families, the best pleasures of life were quite simply not being thirsty, nor hungry, nor cold, nor afraid. A hole in the ground is not a palace, a piece of canvas is not a soft mattress, a sleeping-bag not a warm eiderdown...And yet which of us has not spent divine moments in that hole, on that canvas, in that bag?

Charles Carrington wrote 'If no man...can now guess the meaning of twenty-four hours bombardment, nor has he any notion of ninety-six hours rest. Who has never been drenched and frozen in Flanders mud, has never dreamed of the pleasure derivable from dry blankets on a stone floor.' Paul Lintier, a French artilleryman, summed up the animal satisfaction of those rare moments: 'Ah, how one loves life when one has almost lost it...When danger is, for a moment, at a distance from us, what pleasure there is, with every limb utterly relaxed, to absorb completely oneself in the sweet sensation of being *alive*.'

Convalescent troops resting in a recreation room provided for them by the British Red Cross.

PART FOUR

Attitudes

11 Patriotism and Honour

On, marching men, on
To the gates of death with a song.
Sow your gladness for earth's reaping,
So you may be glad, though sleeping.
Strew your gladness on earth's bed,
So be merry, so be dead.

Charles Sorley

Few men went to the front utterly devoid of any patriotc feelings, a positive sense that what they doing was for the good of their country and that that alone was a worthwhile thing. A young subaltern, J. Engall of the 16th London Regiment, wrote to his parents on the eve of the Battle of the Somme: 'I could not pray for a finer death, and you my dear Mother and Dad, will know that I died doing my duty to my God, my Country and My King.' A French dragoon, Emile Hanriot, wrote in his journal in July 1915: 'One has been able to bear it all and one bears it for what? Because it serves a purpose, it is useful to that entity which is only, in the last analysis, the sum of all things visible and invisible which we most love in the world: *la patrie*.' In 1914 and after such notions had a real meaning, and the thought that one was serving one's country, even to death, had a genuine sustaining effect.

Love of country was bound up in a whole series of obligations that came together under the vague heading of honour and duty. Victorian and Edwardian education and propaganda, the whole ideology of the age, inculcated both officers and men with a real sense of being duty-bound to come forward in the defence of their family, their country, even their country's allies. Many soldiers did not even bother to put their feelings into words; honour was not something that a gentleman talked about. But in their letters home, to close friends and family, many of the men did give expression

British sentry keeping watch while his comrades sleep.

to their most deeply felt feelings. Harold Parry left Oxford to become a lieutenant in the King's Royal Rifles, and just before joining up he wrote to his mother:

> I have no wish to remain a civilian any longer; and, though the whole idea of war is against my conscience, I feel that in a time of national crisis like the present the individual has no right whatever to urge his views if they are contrary to the best and immediate interest of the state.

Another soldier, Alan Thomas, of the 6th Royal West Kents, revealed how binding such notions were within the closed community of a public school: 'I suspect what really moved me [to volunteer] was less a feeling of patriotism than a desire to stand right with my fellows. To have been a conscientious objector at Malvern – even if I had wanted to be one – would have been unthinkable.' By the spring of 1915 over two-thirds of the Oxbridge undergraduates had volunteered for service.

But it was not only the officers who felt this compulsion to do their duty and join up. Public school education no doubt formulated the notion much more precisely, but the ordinary soldiers too felt themselves impelled by some vague sense of obligation, like the dying young Cockney who remembered that: 'I fought I was too big to be walking about the street wivout joining.' In *Her Privates We,* Frederick Manning described a conversation between an officer and a group of NCOs. One of the latter endeavours to explain why he joined up at all: 'When a saw all them as didn' know any better'n we did joining up, an' a went walking out wi' me girl on Sundays, as usual, a just felt ashamed. An' a put it away, an' a put it away, until in th'end it got me down.'

This notion of honour remained with soldiers throughout their service and was a key reason why men chose to endure the agonies of the trenches. R.C. Sherriff served as an officer with the 9th East Surrey Regiment until he was discharged after the Third Battle of Ypres. In his play *Journey's End* he tried to give expression to this sense of personal obligation. A company commander, Stanhope, is trying to reason with an officer who is trying to malinger his way out of the trenches:

> If you went – and left Osborne and Trotter and Raleigh and all those men up there to do your work – could you ever look a man straight in the face again – in all your life? You may be wounded. Then you can go home and feel proud...You're still alive – with a straight fighting chance of coming through. Take the chance, old chap, and stand in with Osborne and Trotter and Raleigh. Don't you think it worth standing in with men like that? – when you know that they all feel like you do – in their hearts – and just go on sticking it because they know it's – it's the only thing a decent man can do. What about it?

What most men feared was fear itself, finding themselves unable to do what they felt was required of them. It was the struggle against any display of personal weakness that kept many of the soldiers going. Though ostensibly motivated by very general considerations like patriotism, the troops fought a very personal war, obsessed almost with a sense of individual honour. A German soldier, Johannes Philippsen, wrote in his diary in July 1917, of the veteran's constant struggle to master his own instinctive fear:

> We, who have seen the dark side, must substitute for that enthusiasm [of the new recruit] a deep-seated determination to stand by the Fatherland whatever happens as long as it has need of us. We know that death is not the worst thing that we have to face. Thoroughly to realise everything and yet to go back, not under compulsion, but willingly, is not easy. To try and deceive oneself by working oneself up into a state of excitement is, I hold, unworthy. Only genuine self-command is any use to me.

German soldiers rotting in the mud.

He did go back willingly and was killed in action on 20 September.

For others, this inward struggle and the victory over fear was the most vivid of their personal impressions, joyfully celebrated in their letters and diaries. A French painter wrote: 'Dear Mother, how shall I ever speak of the unspeakable things I have had to see. But how shall I ever tell of the certainties this tempest has made clear to me? Duty. Effort.' In May 1915 a young British officer of the Leinster Regiment described his victory over fear in his first battle: 'It makes me sing and grin to myself in the dark, and thank God, I believe I can do what is up to me.' Steven Hewett wrote home in May 1916: 'Warm work!...but mark you, I would not be elsewhere for worlds...I loathe it healthily and heartily, but I am sure it is doing me good.' Many found self-fulfilment in doing their duty as Henry Field wrote home to his mother: 'I am much happier than I ever thought I should be in the Army. After all, I am in my destined place, and doing or about to do what I should be doing or about to do...and thank God I don't flinch from the sound of the guns.'

Those with a penchant for putting their feelings into verse, whether good or bad, often tried to describe this same triumph over self. Robert Nichols wrote a poem simply entitled 'Thanksgiving', which expresses just this relief at being able to 'stick it out':

Yet give I thanks; despite these wars,
My ship – though blindly blown,
Long lost to sun or moon or stars –
Still stands up alone.
I need no trust in borrowed spars;
My strength is yet my own.

Nichols, a member of the Royal Artillery, was invalided out of the Army after the Battle of the Some, suffering from shell-shock, from which he never entirely recovered.

For many men this personal affirmation turned into an almost joyful acceptance of death. Rupert Brooke wrote:

Blow out, you bugles, over the rich Dead!
There's none of these so lonely and poor of old,
But, dying, has made us rarer gifts than gold.

Such men invoked death almost longingly, as a means of giving their lives some sense of purpose. W.S. Littlejohn expressed almost a manic compulsion to be killed. In a poem called 'To S–, A Man who Died Bravely', he frames for himself almost a berserker's creed in the face of death:

So there is just a laughing death-song in my heart as
                                                    up I plod
To the trenches, where my need will be six-foot
                                              stretch of sod
With a plain wood cross above it – leave the rest of
                                               me to God.

Such morbid resignation, fascination even, seems to have
helped many soldiers face up to their duties. But this attitude
to death, and the sense of honour and duty well done were
very personalised feelings. They were a reaction to war and
battle in the abstract, rather than any particular enemy.
Despite all the hysterical propaganda from the home front,
few men in the trenches hated those on the other side of the
wire. A French officer, Norton Cru, felt that there was a
reverse correlation between xenophobia and proximity to the
enemy:

German machine gunner
surrenders at the point of a
bayonet. Note the concrete
pillbox.

Hatred of the enemy diminished as one passed from the interior to the front, where it tapered off still more as one went from staffs to field headquarters, from headqarters to batteries, from batteries to the battalion command post, and finally from there to the infantryman in the trench and observation sap, where it reached its lowest ebb.

Or as C.E. Montague put it, rather more tersely: 'War hath no fury like a noncombatant.'

In battle itself, of course, passions were aroused, and many men have described being overcome with a frenzied blood-lust, an overpowering desire to kill and kill again. In one of his best poems, 'The Assault', Robert Nichols attempted to describe his feelings when going over the top. The poem ends as he stumbles over no man's land and encounters the Germans:

> Devouring thought crying in a dream,
> Men crumpled, going down...
> Go on, Go.
> Deafness. Numbness. The loudening tornado.
> Bullets. Mud. Stumbling and skating.
> My voice's strangled shout;
> 'Steady pace, boys!'
> The still light; gladness,
> 'Look, sir! Look out!'
> Ha! Ha! Bunched figures waiting.
> Revolver levelled quick!
> Flick! Flick!
> Red as blood.
> Germans. Germans.
> Good! O good!
> Cool madness.

A member of the British Machine Gun Corps has described his feelings during the Battle of the Somme, after his company had been almost completely wiped out:

> To the south of the wood Germans could be seen, silhouetted against the sky-line, moving forward. I fired at them and watched them fall, chuckling with joy at the technical efficiency of the machine...[Later] anger, and the intensity of the fire, consumed my spirit, and not caring for the consequences, I rose and turned my machine gun upon...[a] battery, laughing loudly as I saw the loaders fall.

Nevertheless such reactions were not typical of the everyday attitude towards the Germans. Even in these cases, in fact, one detects a primitive delight in killing for its own sake rather than a hatred of Germans. In any case one never saw one's enemy for much of the time and the fury of action soon cooled into a grudging sympathy for the other side as Marie-Paul Rimbault wrote: 'There's nothing so like a German soldier in his trench than a French soldier in *his*. They are both poor sods and that's all there is to it.'

When there was not too much pressure from higher commands, both sides were quite prepared to adopt a policy of live and let live. Over the years certain sectors gained a reputation for being especially 'cushy', at least in relative terms. The generals, for various reasons, left them out of their strategic calculations and the troops were left to live life as much like peacetime as possible. This was particularly the case in certain parts of the French line. A stretch of trenches near Hennescamps in late 1915 was occupied by a French territorial battalion, and it was put about that they only kept two sentries in the front line and all fired off their rifles once a week to make sure they were still in working order. The Chemin des Dames Ridge had been the scene of very bitter fighting, but from September 1917 it too became very quiet and German troops were always keen to be posted there, referring to it as the 'sanatorium of the West'. Southern sectors were also quiet, and the French were very upset when American units were moved in there because they insisted on attacking the Germans.

US 1st Division (known as the Big Red One) go over the top in the assault on Cantigny, May 1918. The man in the left foreground is carrying a Vivien-Bessier rifle grenade.

A French soldier commented ruefully: 'When one labours for four years in Artois, at Verdun and other bad sectors, and one has the good fortune to find a quiet and wooded spot, what bad luck to see some idiot excite the sector.'

Even in the most fiercely contested sectors there were moments when the two sides were able to reach a temporary understanding. A basic code was evolved which allowed certain tasks to be undertaken without fear of reprisal. Greenwell wrote in his diary in May 1915 in Ploegsteert Wood: 'The German working parties are also out, so it is not considered etiquette to fire.' In most sectors it was agreed that there would be no shooting for an hour or so during breakfast and dinner. In the Cambrai sector in October 1917 an understanding was reached that one could freely walk about in the trenches, or even on the parados without being shot at by snipers. Individual soldiers, too, often experienced a sudden revulsion at the idea of killing an exposed enemy when the opportunity offered. A Canadian soldier at Kemmel, in November 1915 once found himself a few yards from the German lines after blundering about in the fog. When it lifted he was spotted by a sentry who told him: 'You had better go back or I shall have to shoot you.'

Truces were most common at certain specific periods. One of these was in very bad weather when both sides were totally occupied with the struggle against the elements. In November 1915 Greenwell reported that both sides were bailing out their trenches in full view of one another: 'Our men didn't shoot though ordered to do so.' In February 1915 in various parts of Flanders, both sides came out into the open, and even met in no man's land, without any shots being fired because the trenches were completely flooded. B. Chaney, an NCO in the 7th London Territorial Battalion, remembered that in the vicious winter of 1916-17 both sides lit fires at night in the trenches and openly stamped around on the parapets to try and keep themselves warm. Germans and British ignored one another until a visiting brigadier saw what was happening and took immediate steps to stop it.

Another frequent occasion for these informal cease-fires was the retrieval of the dead and wounded after an attack. A German soldier, Karl Aldag, described such a truce on New Year's Eve 1914 when, according to his account, a British officer crossed no man's land at 3 a.m., and asked for an opportunity to bury his dead. During the next two hours or so the troops on both sides left their trenches and exchanged cigarettes, tins of food and photographs. The German officer in charge became very nervous and insisted on ending this brief respite: 'The [British] officers answered that they were sorry, but their men wouldn't obey orders. They didn't want to go on. The soldiers said they had had enough of lying in wet trenches, and that France was done for.' This story was

probably exaggerated but the point remains that the ordinary soldier was curious to find our what the 'Hun' was really like. These burial truces were quite common. On the first day of the Battle of the Somme, German stretcher-bearers came out at certain points, under white flags, and picked up British wounded near their own wire. In August 1916 Australian stretcher-bearers came out, carrying Red Cross flags, and the Germans did not recommence firing until the battlefield had been cleared. The Australians then reciprocated. In February 1917 the 1st Civil Service Rifles and a German unit came to a similar agreement. Shortly afterwards they received a directive from Divisional Headquarters: 'We have to deal with a treacherous and unscrupulous foe, who, from the commencement of the present war, has repeatedly proved himself unworthy of the slightest confidence. No commuication is to be held with him without definite instructions from Divisional HQ...'

Sometimes these brief lulls in the fighting were quite impromptu, at the most unexpected times. They often took the form of recitals, as one man or a small group on one side played or sang some tune and were suddenly aware, from the applause at the end, that the enemy had been listening. Then,

British and German troops fraternising on Christmas day, 1914.

as often as not, the listeners would give some rendition of their own. Philip Gibbs tells how, during a pause in the savage fighting at Loos, a British Guards battalion gave a concert in the front-line trenches, with mouth-organs, combs and paper and penny-whistles. The Germans applauded each number and at one stage a voice shouted across, in English 'Play "Annie Laurie" and I will sing it.' They did and a German officer stood on the parapet and sang the song. There was applause on both sides. The next day battle was resumed 'and the young officers of the Guards told the story as an amusing anecdote with loud laughter'.

The most famous example of fraternisation on the Western Front was on Christmas Day 1914. Then, up and down the whole line, Frenchmen, Germans and Englishmen spontaneously emerged from their trenches and met in no man's land where they exchanged cigarettes, drink, food, photographs and addresses. A company of the 2nd Battalion Lancashire Fusiliers even played a game of football with a Saxon unit, which they won 3-2. Many soldiers were surprised to find that their enemy seemed quite human. An officer of the London Rifle Brigade wrote: 'They were really magnificent in the whole thing, and jolly good sorts. I now have a very different opinion of the Germans.' Sir Edward Hulse was struck by the unreality of the whole affair:

> Meanwhile Scots and Huns were fraternising in the most genuine manner possible. Every sort of souvenir was exchanged, addresses given and received, photos of families shown... A German NCO started his fellows off in some marching tune. When they had done I set the note for 'The Boys of Bonnie Scotland', and so we went on singing everything from 'Good King Wenceslas' to the ordinary Tommy's song, and ended up with 'Auld Land Syne' which we all, English, Scots, Irish, Prussians, Wurtenbergers, etc., joined in. It was absolutely astounding, and if I had seen it on a cinematograph film I should have sworn that it was faked.

But when news of these meetings reached the High Command they were utterly appalled at the seeming disintegration of the 'fighting spirit'. Sir John French wrote afterwards that he had heard tell of

> ...unarmed men running from the German trenches across to ours holding Christmas trees above their heads. These overtures were in some places favourably received and fraternisation of a limited kind took place...When this was reported to me, I issued immediate orders to prevent any recurrence of such conduct, and called the local commanders to strict account, which resulted in a good deal of trouble.

In the following years strict orders were given that all efforts by the enemy to fraternise were to be sternly resisted. On 25 December 1915 a slow artillery barrage was laid down during the whole day. Captain Hitchcock cited the orders that he received in the following year, from Battalion HQ: 'With the intention of showing the enemy that we have no intention of fraternising with him, and also with a view to taking advantage of any slackness on his part over Christmas, a special programme will be carried out by the Artillery, T[rench] M[ortar]s and Machine Guns.'

12 Disillusionment and Protest

But War, — as war is now, and always was:
A dirty, loathesome, servile murder-job:—
Men, lousy, sleepless, ulcerous, afraid,
Toiling their hearts out in the pulling slime
That wrenches gum-boot down from bleeding heel
And cakes in itching arm-pits, navel, ears:
Men stunned to brainlessness, and gibbering:
Men driving men to death and worse than death:
Men maimed and blinded: men against machines —
Flesh versus iron, concrete, flame and wire:
Men choking out their souls in poison gas:
Men squelched into the slime by trampling feet:
Men, disembowelled by guns five miles away,
Cursing, with their last breath, the living God
Because He made them, in His image, men...

Gilbert Frankau

Duty, rather than chauvinism sustained many men during their years at the Front. But though this helped men stick it out, it generated no enthusiasm. As the war dragged on disillusionment spread. Soldiers who had been there for a long time reacted against the constant strain, and the older men called up in the third and fourth years of the war were hardly able to endure the rigours of front-line service. This gradual erosion of the will to persevere is apparent in the letters and diaries of many soldiers. In May 1915 Charles Greenwell felt able to write: 'It is all so delightfully fresh after England that the unpleasant side of it doesn't strike me, though all my friends have been trying to instil into me the gospel of frightfulness.' Some months later he wrote: 'I shall never look on warfare as fine or sporting again. It reduces men to shivering beasts.' An even more striking contrast is afforded by the letters of an anonymous doctor who volunteered for the front. An early communication ends on a purely enthusiastic note: 'Now I really must stop, but I must say that I am having the time of my life. Sounds odd, but it's true. I only hope that nothing happens to turn me out unless it happens to be a Bosch bullet, and that could not be helped.' Again within a few months he had joined those countless men whose dearest wish was for a 'Blighty wound': 'I am getting so played up that I don't know what will happen, that is unless I have the luck to get a Blighty this evening. I have been hoping for a mild one; the only thing I did get was that rotten little thing in my leg; no earthly good.'

For many men the essence of their disenchantment was the

Exhausted stretcher-bearers catch a moment's rest during the fighting before Passchendaele.

stark contrast between their image of the glories of war and the reality they encountered. Captain T.C. Wilson of the Sherwood Foresters was quite explicit:

> All those picturesque phrases of war writers...are dangerous because they show nothing of the individual horror, nothing of the fine personalities suddenly smashed into red beastliness, nothing of the sick fear that is tearing at the hearts of brave boys...a thing infinitely more terrible than physical agony.

Even a divisional history, normally a document which prized stiff-upper-lip understatement above everything else, gave a most moving description of the progressive demoralisation of the troops. By the end of the Third Battle of Ypres

> ...the secrecy and furtiveness of every movement, the ghastliness of the abomination of desolation all around...combined to awaken a vague inarticulate protest against the cruelty and futility of war...Depression [was] generated by a sense of impotence – the beating of one's head against a concrete wall, the waste of effort and lives thrown away in futile local assaults.

Sassoon's poetry makes much of the contrast between imagined glories and the sordid reality. In poem after poem he builds up a dramatic tension and then destroys it, refusing to let us escape into false sentimentality. In 'The Redeemer' Sassoon believes for a moment that he has seen a vision of the crucified Christ in the gloom of a trench. Then the figure comes nearer:

> And someone flung his burden in the muck,
> Mumbling: 'O Christ Almighty, now I'm stuck.'

The thoughtless blasphemy, the ugly rhyme of the last couplet, the banality of the muttered curse combine to jolt the reader out of any complacent visions of heroics and adventurous derring-do.

It is very difficult to establish the exact degree of disillusionment. But it is clear that there were many who hated what was going on, and these were not simply a minority of 'over-sensitive' intellectuals. Both enthusiasm and disenchantment existed side by side. In a poem by A.G. West, they actually confront each other as he curses those who cheerfully go to their death believing that it was 'happy to have lived these epic days'.

And *he'd* been to France,
And seen the trenches, glimpsed the huddled dead
In the periscope, hung in the rustling wire:
Choked by their sickly foetor, day and night
Blown down his throat: stumbled through ruined hearths,
Proved all that muddy brown monotony,
Where blood's the only coloured thing. Perhaps
Had seen a man killed, a sentry shot at night,
Hunched as he fell, his feet on the firing-step,
His neck against the back slope of the trench,
And the rest doubled up between, his head
Smashed like an egg-shell, and warm grey brain
Spattered all bloody on the parados:

In July 1918 the British Censorship Department sent a report
to Haig trying to analyse the state of the men's morale
through their letters home. The Report was fairly emphatic
that the great majority of letters revealed no real sense of
defeatism or despair. But whatever the exact proportion of
discontented men many men had almost had enough. While
one could write: 'Really, I am so proud to be a British soldier
and to be able to fight to the bitter end for British interest, and
it is the same with all of us out here', another reported that,
'Everybody is fed up with the war out here and doesn't care
who wins so long as we can get it over.'

One probable reason for this complete difference of opinion
was the wide age-range of those in France, towards the end of
the war. As the manpower shortage became more acute older

Artillery men 'as keen as
mustard' after a heavy day at
the guns.

and older men were pushed into the front line to fell the gaps. 'The kind of life they were called upon to live was so widely outside anything they could have imagined that they couldn't get on terms with it...it was sheer, abominable cruelty to hurl such men as these into the brutal, amphibious life of the front-line infantry.' In November 1917 T.S. Hope noticed: 'The youngsters are as keen as mustard, and take to the new procedure as if it was some game they were being instructed in, but with the older men it is different. They have no enthusiasm, and give the impression of being here much against their will, and so I suppose they are.' But age was not the only factor. There was a definite decline in British morale over the four years of war. The early enthusiasm gave way to a glum resignation. An early volunteer gave anonymous but sardonic expression to his own war-weariness:

It must be so – it's wrong to doubt
The voluntary system's best.
Your conscript, when you've dug him out,
Has not the Happy Warrior's zest.
Because it seemed the thing to do
I joined with other volunteers
But – well, I don't mind telling you
I didn't reckon for three years.
Though we observe the Higher Law
And though we have our quarrel just,
Were I permitted to withdraw
You wouldn't see my arse for dust.

Private Chaney felt that the Somme battle, with its bloody sense of anti-climax, was the turning point: 'From now on the veterans, myself included, decided to do no more than was really necessary, following orders, but if possible keeping out of harm's way. I have the feeling that many of the officers felt the same way.' A Canadian artilleryman echoed very similar sentiments as he remembered the long sequence of bloody stalemates he had been involved in: 'Butchering the poor bloody infantry and knocking the light artillery to pieces... We who had long service became similar to dumb animals, obeyed orders, no longer caring what happened.' General Pershing, in command of the American Expeditionary Force wrote in July 1918: 'The morale of the Allies is low and association with them has a bad effect on our men.' R.H. Mottram felt that the Third Battle of Ypres was a very decisive turning point:

The miserable failure of an offensive was brought to a close. But the effect was permanent. From this time there developed a new spirit of taking care of oneself among the men, which ended, in late 1918, in few rifles being fired, and would, in a few more weeks, have meant the cessation of the war, by the front line not refusing but quietly omitting to do duty. The Armistice came just in time.

Yet, in the British Army at least, this disillusionment hardly ever flared up into open mutiny. Army discipline remained intact. Most of the major disturbances occurred right at the end of the war, many of them after the Armistice itself, when the troops felt that they were not being demobilised quickly enough. In 1918 at Calais between 21 and 26 July the 51st Highland Division rioted and many military policemen were thrown into the sea before the troops were finally brought to order. On the 9 and 10 December, units of the Royal Artillery burnt down some of the depots and between 21 and 27 December troops at the Tank Corps workshops went on strike. In January 1919 there was another big strike at Calais Base, the troops protesting over the arrest of a private of the Royal Army Ordnance Corps, John Pantling, who was supposed to have made a seditious speech to his comrades. A doctor reported that after the Armistice 'robbery reached surprising lengths in Belgium. Numbers of motor cars were stolen, and supply trains were robbed by men in uniform, who got into the wagons at night and threw the contents to their confederates whilst the train was on the move.'

The most important disturbance during the hostilities themselves again took place in a Base Area, at Etaples, fifteen miles south of Boulogne. Conditions there were spartan and both fresh units from England and those recuperating after a spell in the line underwent a strenuous training programme in the so-called 'Bull Ring'. A corporal remembers meeting several when returning to the front with wounds which were far from healed. 'When I asked why they had returned in that condition they invariably replied: "To get away from the Bull Ring".' Rioting broke out on 9 September when military policemen guarding a bridge that led from the training areas into town clashed with a large crowd of soldiers forcing their

British troops going on parade at the Bull Ring, Etaples.

way into the town and breaking into the *estaminets*. Henry Williamson has left a vivid account of what happened:

> The mutiny had begun with the organised defiance of orders at the Bull Ring; the streaming back of thousands of men singing and cheering; the shooting of the sergeant of the Gordon Highlanders * by an NCO of the Military Field Police...The General had tried to address them – 'Are you Englishmen, or are you blackguards?' – and had been told to put a sock in it...Then the hunt of the red-caps through Etapps; the looting of the *estaminets*... Some said that junior officers had been disguised as private soldiers in order to get into the *estaminets* and spot the organisers of the mutiny; after them had come the break-up patrols armed with entrenching tool handles, laying out the leaders when found. A posh battalion of territorials from GHQ; machine guns on the bridge over the river; no food...Dozens of poor sods handcuffed wrist to wrist, two by two...awaiting court martial and the firing squad. That was the end of that!

In fact, as far as is known, no one was shot, the authorities being acutely aware that such action could well provoke even more serious disturbances which might even spread to the front line.

In the French and German armies the situation became much more critical. In the German lines the gradual deterioration of morale hastened the final collapse. At first there was only the same kind of exhaustion experienced in the British Army. After the Battle of Passchendaele Rudolph Binding wrote: 'One cannot say that the *morale* is low or weak. The regiments simply show a sort of staggering and faltering, as people do who have made unheard efforts.' But as supplies from the home front dried up and the increasing strength of the Americans became apparent, things slowly got out of hand, although many German soldiers did not realise until the very end that time was running out.

The High Command was well aware of the situation. In August 1918 the Crown Prince issued an order which noted that

> In the heavy fighting of the last two months, the great and continuous strain on officers and men, and to a certain extent the arrival of inadequately trained drafts, have led at times to a slackening of discipline which is betrayed in the bearing of the troops. I attach all the greater importance to the maintenance of iron discipline, because the long duration of the war, with its accompanying phenomena at and behind the front, are unquestionably exercising disintegrating influences in this sphere too

---

*In fact, Corporal W.B. Wood of the 4th Battalion.

In the second half of 1918 Ludendorff wrote: 'As our best men became casualties our infantry approximated more nearly in character to a militia and discipline declined.' The new recruits of the last year of the war certainly had much to do with it. Many of the young had been radicalised by the political and economic situation at home and brought with them subversive ideas and literature. Even the release of troops from the Eastern Front, after Brest-Litovsk, proved a mixed blessing. There war-weariness had reached a peak and fraternisation had taken place on a scale unparalleled on the Western Front. One entire trainload of troops refused to go to the front on their arrival in Belgium. Desertions increased. At least 4,000 German troops were interned in neutral Holland between September 1916 and the Armistice, whilst in the last three months of the war 40,000 soldiers voluntarily gave themselves up to the American forces. Ludendorff wrote: 'The troops had borne the continuous defensive with extreme difficulty. Skulkers were already numerous. They reappeared as soon as the battle was over, and it had become quite common for divisons which came out of action with desperately low effectives to be considerably stronger after only a few days [in rest].

It is, however, debatable whether the Germans would have been able to resist the renewed Allied offensives even if their troops had been in perfect condition. The balance of manpower and *matériel* was too much against them. For the French, on the other hand, war-weariness provoked a series of mutinies which almost destroyed their armies as a viable fighting force. By April 1917 the French Army was almost completely exhausted. The casualty figures had reached an unparalleled climax in Nivelle's futile Champagne offensive of April 1917. For many units leave had effectively ceased and conditions in the rest areas, when the troops eventually got there, were becoming increasingly bad. Pétain wrote of the troops at this time: 'The French Army was exhausted. Hopelessness and pessimism spread to it from the interior, swamping as it did so the mood of artificial enthusiasm, whipped up from above...The fighting troops were at the end of their tether.' There had been isolated acts of protest in the previous years. In November 1915, for example, the 3rd Battalion of the 63rd Infantry Regiment had refused to go over the top at Vimy. The whole battalion was court-martialled and one man from every company sentenced to be shot. This scapegoat was selected by the company commander who drew a number out of a hat. Desertions became more and more frequent. At the beginning of the war the authorities had calculated that as many as thirteen per cent of those called up might refuse to join the colours, though the actual figure was only 1.5 per cent and there were only 409 desertions during the rest of the year. But in 1915 the figure was 2,433; in 1916 it

French troops marching to the front.

was almost 9,000; and in 1917, 21,871 men deserted. In May 1917 these individual acts of protest coalesced into a general movement. On 29 April the 18th Infantry Regiment had refused to leave its rest area to go to the front. It was only prevailed upon to move forward after the arrest of several ringleaders and the passing of five death sentences, four of which were carried out. On 3 May the 2nd Colonial Infantry Division appeared on parade prior to their departure for the notorious Chemin des Dames Ridge. Suddenly the officers became aware that the men had neither packs nor rifles, and when asked why anonymous voices shouted 'We're not marching', 'Down with the War' and 'We're not such fools as to attack against uncut barbed wire or unshelled German trenches'. Eventually the officers managed to cajole the men to move up the line, but only on the understanding that they would not have to attack. This was a common feature of the mutinies that followed. The troops assured their officers that they would not let the Germans pass, but they adamantly refused to take part in any more futile assaults.

After this the movement quickly spread. By the end of May it was estimated that only two out of the twelve division in Champagne could be relied upon, and none of those between Paris and Soissons. In all seventy-five regiments of infantry, twenty-three battalions of chausseurs and twelve regiments of artillery were tainted by mutinies which reached their zenith between 1 and 3 June.

The movement was essentially a straightforward mutiny not a political struggle. Though the soldiers often adopted some of the rhetoric and formal trappings of pre-war French Radicalism and the Russian Revolution – the 'Internationale' was sung and certain units elected their own deputies or officers on the line of the Russian Soldiers' Councils – their basic demands were concerned with their actual situation at the front. They assumed that the war would go on, were prepared to carry on fighting to drive the invader out, and only asked that certain of the grosser abuses affecting their army life, leave, rest, medical services and so on be put right.

The mutinies were put down with a mixture of brute force and concessions. Pétain, who was given charge of bringing the army back to order, made a point of visiting every division, addressing the men and holding discussions with both senior and junior officers. Tactics were changed: limited attacks were backed by maximum artillery support; the infantry were to operate in small, dispersed groups and avoid the old attack *en masse*. Training in these new methods was immediately stepped up. Defence in depth, with only a very thinly held front line, was emphasised, as well as a much more regular rotation between front-line and reserve formations. On 2 June all troops were guaranteed seven days leave every four months, later extended to ten days. The food was greatly improved. Pétain insisted on a hundred lorry-loads of fresh vegetables a day, as well as the setting-up of regimental co-operatives where men could buy extra provisions at the lowest prices. The rest areas were also improved. Where possible, men were to spend half their time at rest and never less than a fortnight on each occasion. On 3 August an order was placed for the immediate delivery of 400,000 beds into the rest zones.

Although Pétain also revoked the special courts-martial which had been able to sentence mutineers to death without prior reference to the Minister of War, he did not shrink from using the sternest disciplinary measures to put down the

mutinies. Nearly 24,000 men were court-martialled and many of them were shipped off to colonies almost immediately. This abrupt disappearance of whole units gave rise to rumours of mass executions. These are now generally accepted not to have taken place, though some men certainly were shot after hastily convened courts-martial, and even more executed out of hand by those units, usually the cavalry, called in physically to restrain the more mutinous regiments. We shall never know exactly how many. Painlevé said twenty-three, Pé fifty-three, but neither of them were in a position to count.

For most of the war indiscipline was not a great problem in any of the armies. Even the French mutinies only lasted for two months, and the German breakdown only came at the very end of the hostilities. In the British Army, 169,040 officers and men appeared before courts-martial, which represents about 3.5 per cent of the total numer of soldiers who served. This does not include those who appeared before their company commander or commanding officer, but this was always for relatively trivial offences. The most common charges in courts-martial were absence without leave with 37,034 cases and drunkenness with 35,313. Indiscipline and insubordination, amounted to 22,891 cases. Mutiny only accounts for 1,132 cases, desertion for 7,361, cowardice for 551 and self-inflicted wounds for 3,894 – together less than one per cent of the total number of men in France. According to the official figures only 322 of these were shot; seventy-eight per cent of them for desertion. Although it is certain that some men were shot out of hand by their officers in critical situations.

Of course these figures do not tell the whole story, particularly as regards desertion and cowardice. They only represent the people who were charged and there were various reasons why a man might avoid this. Certain deserters were never caught, even though they remained behind the British lines. The woods near Etaples were supposed to be full of them, obtaining food and money by silently sand-bagging passing travellers. Certain soldiers deserted to the Germans, J.F.C. Fuller told the Shell Shock Enquiry of 1922 that the Battle of Ancre in 1916 'was the only battle of which I had direct evidence that British troops deserted in considerable numbers to the enemy'. Sometimes the offence involved too many troops for the authorities to be able to do much about it. This is a basic principle of military discipline. If a few individuals, or a platoon or company breaks, disciplinary action is possible. The men are exceptions to the rule, and everyone, even they themselves, can see some justice in their punishment. Also sufficient men can be found to do the rounding up. But if a whole battalion or brigade should crack then the High Command is virtually powerless to do anything about it. This happened on several occasions in the British forces during the First World War. During the Battle of Mons, Aubrey Herbert of the Irish Guards witnessed the flight of an unnamed regiment which had lost all its officers, and whose men rushed back through the Guards' own ranks. A few of Herbert's own men were infected by the panic but, as he tersely put it: 'This was put right at once.' At the Battle of Loos, the whole of the 21st and 24th Divisions retreated and there were may instances of hysterical, uncontrollable men smashing their rifles as they fled back. In November 1917 the 12th Divison broke and fled during the German counter-attack that followed the initial successes at the Battle of Cambrai. There were more than a few such instances during the German offensive of early 1918. On 22 March the 15th and 16th Battalions of the Royal Scots broke when, already severely mauled by the German artillery, their lines

One of the survivors after the battle for Beaumont Hamel.

were also hit by British shells. They were only rallied in the third line of defence by the personal example of a lieutenant-colonel and a major. Frank Dunham described the demeanour of many of the units of the Fourth Army that he encountered during the British retreat:

On every face was a kind of hopeless look, nowhere did I discern a smile, and to my eyes, at that time, it certainly looked like a rout. It seemed everyone's aim was to get as far away as possible from the battle, and it was surprising how soon after being among this crowd, we appeared to be obsessed with the same idea.

The High Command was certainly awake to the possibility that the troops might try and get away from the battle zone. During the Third Battle of Ypres an order was given that any man found behind Battalion HQ after zero hour for an attack was automatically to face a Field General Court Martial. Battle Police were also employed to prevent soldiers getting to the rear. Most privates were not sure whether they existed or not. But General Jack's orders in 1917 make explicit mention of the Provost-Sergeant and the Battalion Police being posted in the front trenches to arrest any man who might return improperly during an attack.

Malingerers were even present in the American Army, whose naive and unabashed patriotic zeal was the wonder of their allies. General Liggett wrote afterwards of the 1st US Army during the Meuse-Argonne offensive:

Some evidences [sic] of discouragement were beginning to appear among both men and officers, the most conspicuous evidence of which was the great number of stragglers...[many merely got lost] but there were others in numbers of stragglers who were 33rd-degree brothers in the ancient order of AWOL, men who had shirked every possible duty from the day they had first reported at camp...Actual desertion was negligible, in no small part because the Atlantic Ocean discouraged it.

T.S. Hope wrote of the continual rumours of units mutinying or breaking:

Then a brigade...on our right, who seem to have got tired of the whole business, packed up and retreated...How we enjoy trying to believe these rumours. The only disturbing factor is we can never find an eye-witness to any of them. It is always a battalion on our left, a brigade on our right, a machine-gunner who has a brother who knows someone in the Intelligence Department or...a batman who passed the officers' latrines...

W.A. Tucker of the 38th (Welsh) Divisional Cyclist Company was even more to the point: 'Did it often happen that our men broke down under bombardment, desert, or show cowardice? No, it didn't …In three years up front I personally never saw a single instance…I have seen men pale with fright – I have been that way myself – but I never saw a man run the other way.'

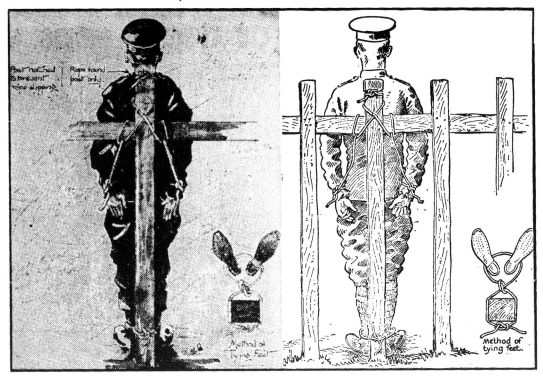

Two versions of Field Punishment Number 1, popularly known as the 'Cruxifiction'. The picture on the left shows it as it was in reality, the one on the right as it appeared in the War Office Manuals.

13 Conclusion

They lived in a world which is as different from this known world of ours as though they belonged to another race of men inhabiting another planet.

Philip Gibbs

We're here because we're here because
We're here because we're here
We're here because we're here because
We're here because we're here…

Soldiers' song, sung to the tune of 'Auld Lang Syne'.

In the war as a whole, on all sides, most men simply did what they conceived to be their duty. When they were told to hold, they held; when told to advance, they went forward even to almost certain death. The reasons for this lay in their sense of patriotism, duty, honour and deference to authority; all much more important concepts than they are today. But there was something more than this, something that owed little to the pre-conceptions and habits born of pre-war life. The situation the soldiers were in created a logic of its own, its own inherent pressures to force men to carry on to the bitter end. For the men were cut off from the world they had known, and plunged into an utterly alien environment. The Western Front became a self-contained nightmare whose rules and traditions became ends in themselves, the only thing a man could cling on to in the midst of chaos. This sense of isolation generated the collective pride that helped them endure because it drew the soldiers so closely together. But what made the soldiers feel so utterly cut off?

For some, there was the growing conviction that the war might never end. This led to the deepest fits of gloom, a horrible sense of futility in which time bore down on the shoulders like a dead weight. The word 'boredom' crops up again and again in the memoirs of the time, but it was something much more than the lethargic impatience of someone with time to kill; it was, rather, a spiritual vacuum. T.M. Kettle of the Dublin Fusiliers referred to the war as 'The Long Endurance' and tried to hint at the true nature of this wearisomeness: 'In the trenches it is the day-by-dayness that tells and tries. It is always the same tone of duty...And of course the nerve-strain is not slight...In the trenches death is random, illogical, devoid of principle.' Captain Manwaring felt that his grip on reality was graually slipping away and was aware of an increasing uncertainty about his own place in what was happening. In one of his letters he described how: 'Often as I sit in the lonely night vigils I look up suddenly and wonder if this can be real or whether I am not asleep and dreaming some strangely impossible dream. Reality is seldom with me these days, and all is lost in a vagueness in this life, where hour after hour drags by; where a day may seem a year from dullness...' A German artillery officer wrote: 'You think a lot about the war; it was actually intended only to be a sort of intermezzo in one's life, and now it will soon have lasted three years, and sometimes everything seems like a bad dream, but one that we have to dream for years and years.' The French had a special word, *le cafard*, to describe the depressive state into which men often sunk. Another artillery officer, Paul Lintier, left a particularly good description of it:

There are days of uncurable depression. It seizes one suddenly, fetter one...one doesn't know why...and it is this that makes this gloomy feeling the more unsettling…a deep-seated, indefinable, indescribable malaise…waiting for some misfortune. One doesn't know what it will be. It's one more misery amongst so many miseries. One calls that *le cafard*.

This sense of boredom was bound up with the men's attempts to make it all mean something and so to see the possibility of an end to it all. When this attempt failed, and the soldiers were crushed by the enormity of the war, then they lost hope and the days and years seemed to stretch ahead into an infinity of futile endeavour. As a German officer, captured during the Battle of the Somme, put it: 'This war was not made in any sense by mankind. We are under a spell.' Wilfred Wilson Gibson, rejected four times by the medical boards before he managed to enlist as a private, took this feeling of unreality and personal helplessness to its logical conclusion:

> They ask me where I've been,
> And what I've done and seen
> But what can I reply,
> Who knows it wasn't I,
> But someone just like me,
> Who went across the sea,
> And with my head and hands
> Killed men in foreign lands…
> Though I must bear the blame
> Because he bore my name.

How the German home front saw their trenches: 'comfortable and ever pleasant trenches'.

In their letters home, soldiers at the front were usually reticent about describing conditions as they really were. As the war progressed this reticence began to express itself as a positive dislike of the home front *as a whole*. The soldiers' sense of isolation was increased and they realised that no one who had not been there could begin to understand what they were having to suffer, and, even worse, that many people at home did not even seem to care. The troops came to feel more and more cut off from pre-war life and withdrew more and more into their own doomed fellowship. Henri Barbusse wrote of this growing schism between home life and existence in the trenches. One of the privates in his squad suddenly bursts out, as the troops are trying to make the most of a brief rest period: 'It isn't one single country, that's not possible. There are two. We're divided into foreign countries. The Front, over there, where there are too many unhappy, and the Rear, here, where there are too many happy.' Many British soldiers felt this

A romanticised propaganda photograph of life in the British lines produced for the home front.

same gulf, perhaps even more so because of the physical barrier of the Channel. Certainly they had reason to do so. Many in England showed an amazing ignorance of what life was like for their soldiers. Unit commanders received a never-ending stream of requests from dead men's relatives tartly demanding to know what had happened to their watches, money, etc. Few people in France or Germany seemed to be any better informed. A letter was found on a dead German soldier, from his sister, which commiserated with him on the fact that: 'You must be terribly tired when you get back to the barracks after the fighting.' French soldiers received letters from solicitous old women, full of questions such as: 'But when it's raining you surely don't fight?' and 'Is there any fighting on Sundays?' Even those that were aware of the trench system imagined 'a front made of concrete, everywhere organised, wth comfortable, even pleasant, trenches.'

This complete lack of understanding led to estrangement and bitterness. Sydney Rogerson described how he wished he were a painter so that he could show 'the talkers, the preachers and the shirkers at home what they were missing, and how little they could ever understand of our feelings, our hopes and our fears.' Paul Nash *was* a painter and he had just the same ambition. In one impassioned outburst he spoke of his desire to convey the truth about the ghastly desolation he saw about him:

It is unspeakable, godless, hopeless. I am no longer an artist interested and curious, I am a messenger who will bring

Life in the French trenches as characterised by the Parisian magazine *L'Illustration.*

Scottish troops awaiting a counter attack.

back word from the men who are fighting to those who want the war to go on for ever. Feeble, inarticulate, will be my message, but it will have a bitter truth, and may it burn their lousy souls.

The complete lack of understanding between soldiers and civilians was never more apparent than when the troops went to England on leave. As the war went on more and more soldiers came back to France extremely disillusioned with the incomprehension, even boredom, which characterised their reception. An officer returned to Greenwell's battalion in March 1916: 'Like most of us, he seems rather disgusted with the general public at home, who don't seem to take any interest in anything much and are frankly bored by the war.' In October 1916 a remarkable letter appeared in the *Nation*, in which an anonymous writer tried to explain to the civilian public why the ordinary soldier felt so alienated from everyday life in England:

JUST BEFORE THE BATTLE, MOTHER (2).
Farewell, Mother, you may never, you may never, Mother,
   Press me to your heart again ;
But oh, you'll not forget me, Mother, you will not forget me,
   If I'm numbered with the slain.

A typical example of the maudlin post cards produced on the home front.

It is very nice to be home again. Yet am I at home? One sometimes doubts it. There are occasions when I feel like a visitor amongst strangers whose intentions are kindly, but whose modes of thought I neither altogether understand nor altogether approve...And your ignorance as to the sentiments of your relations about it!

These soldiers managed, on the whole, to conceal their bitterness and to accept the situation stoically, or gently try and point out where the differences lay. Others were less reticent. On the German side, Rudolph Binding wrote scathingly of the pathetic little gifts which came from home for the front-line troops. Referring to those who actually brought the gifts as as 'novelty-mongering, snobbish busy-bodies', he said: 'The fact that they make their appearance with a thousand packages of bad cigars, indifferent chocolates, and woollies of problematical usefulness seems to make them think that they have a right to have the war shown to them like a leather factory.'

Although the ordinary soldiers felt the chasm between them and those at home just as keenly, theirs was more of a sad resignation, a weary acknowledgement that they were alone, and that only they knew of the horrendous trials that faced them. Charles Sorley came to share this sense of isolation. In one of his poems he speaks of the exclusivity of death, and denies to families and loved ones the right to reclaim even the memory of those that had died:

When you see millions of the mouthless dead
Across your dreams in pale battalions go...
Then, scanning all the o'ercrowded mass, should you
Perceive one face that you loved heretofore.
It is a spook. None wears the face you knew.
Great death has made all his for evermore.

Yet the more men felt estranged from their old way of life, the more they turned to each other for support and consolation. Over the years, there grew up in all the armies on the Western Front an *esprit de corps,* a pride in and loyalty to one's unit, that has scarcely ever been surpassed. Graves wrote of this when describing a discussion in the officers' mess. Although there were many points of disagreement about the relative virtues of drill, leadership, musketry, 'all were agreed that regimental pride remained the strongest moral force that kept a battalion going as an effective fighting unit; contrasting it particularly with patriotism and religion'. Charles Carrington spoke also of soldiers' loyalty to their divisions, the largest formation with which it was possible to identify, as divisions were moved willy-nilly from one Corps to another:

Rarely did you move outside the divisional area or meet men of other divisions. Embracing the *esprit de corps* of the battalion, that link which was so deep-seated that men were so shy about it, so shy that they didn't give it an English name, the divisional spirit was the strongest influence.

Such assertions are not just romantic fancies. In 1915, for example, the War Office ordered that all Territorial battalions with a strength of less than 400 men, and there were many, should amalgamate with one another. There was widespread protest and Sir John French swiftly had to rescind the order. In at least two battalions there was something like a general mutiny.

Yet this feeling of common identity was not just limited to battalion and division. There was a definite sense of comradeship that united the whole army. They were the ones who were doing a task that people at home could not even understand. The very intensity of their suffering gave the soldiers a strange sense of pride, welded them together as a community of martyrs with their own rituals and ways of thinking. At the end of his letter, the anonymous writer to the *Nation* highlighted this sense of uniqueness: 'We see things which you can only imagine. We are strengthened by reflections which you have abandoned...Our background is the same. It is that of August to November 1914. We are your ghosts.'

But the men's feelings towards one another went further than just loyalty to their unit and pride in the achievements of the army. There was also love for one's comrades. The word is not used carelessly. Nothing else can describe the devotion and selflessness that characterised the relationship of men within the same platoon or company. The utter brutality of the surroundings brought out a correspondingly wholehearted compassion for those with whom one was enduring them. Nor was this love only between men and men or officers and officers. It cut right across barriers of rank, and the officer's solicitude towards the men under him was only equalled by many of the soldiers' concern for their leaders' safety.

But this only applied to those actually in the line, to the select brotherhood of the damned who had to suffer all the miseries of trench warfare. Staff officers, in particular, were universally disliked. The main reason for this was that the Staff hardly ever made an appearance at the front and had no conception of the conditions in which their abstract plans expected men to fight. In August 1917 C.D. Baker-Carr of the

British and French troops playing poker behind the lines.

Tank Corps delivered a lecture in which he maintained that fighting on in the Third Battle of Ypres was pointless. He was severely reprimanded for this by Brigadier-General John Davidson, Haig's Director of Operations. In a brief conversation Baker-Carr pointed out that the physical conditions made further fighting almost impossible. Davidson replied that things could not be as bad as that. Baker-Carr asked, 'Have you ever been there yourself?' 'No.' 'Has anyone in OA been there?' 'No.'

Often it was more than the simple ignorance of the Staff that prompted the men's contempt. Leonard Smith of the 12th Canadian Field Ambulance took part in the fighting on Vimy Ridge in March 1917: 'On one journey back with wounded he passed the remnants of a cellar which contained, according to him, four staff officers. They said: "Keep moving, you'll draw fire." Smith's comment on this incident is unprintable.' Captain Essame of the Northamptonshire Regiment was equally forthright: 'After the middle of August 1917 there was a growing distrust of the staff. It would be not too much to say that we hated them.'

But such sentiments were not at all typical of the men's attitudes to the ordinary line officers, who they knew had to share almost the same privations and miseries. As long as an officer was competent his men were prepared to follow him almost anywhere. On numerous occasions men would risk their lives in no man's land to try and bring back a wounded officer or even simply his body. This deep affection was given to any officer who was prepared to share the same dangers as the men. A lance-corporal, A. Laird, felt that he had to write to the wife of Brigadier-General Frank Maxwell, commander of the 27th Infantry Brigade, when the latter was killed whilst touring the front:

> He sat for about two minutes, then he got up again to show what he was saying to the captain, and was just opening his mouth when he got shot. I caught him as he was falling and jumped into a shell hole with him. I held his head against my breast till it was all over. Madam, I cried till my heart was liking to burst.

Edmund Blunden recalled the kindness and generosity of his men in a poem called 'The Watchers', written after the war. He remembers a sentry's concern for his safety as he was making a night inspection of the line:

> When will that stern, fine 'Who goes there?'
> Meet me again in midnight air?
> And the gruff sentry's kindness, when
> Will kindness have such power again?

It is difficult to find many specific examples of the ordinary soldier's attitude to his officers simply because so few of them have left records of their experiences, and anyway it was a thing about which most men were very reticent. But the officers' memoirs do, again and again, make mention of their very close identification with the men in their platoon or company. It was the men's capacity for endurance that impressed so many of their officers. Captain Campbell wrote:

> There is one cheering thing. The men of the battalion – through all...through the wet, cold night, hungry and tired, living now in mud and water, with every prospect of more rain tomorrow – are cheery. Sometimes, back in billets, I hate the men...But in a difficult time they show up splendidly. Laughing in mud, joking in water.

In a letter to his wife, Lieutenant-Colonel Rowland Fielding was even more admiring:

> I can never express in writing what I feel about the men in the trenches; and nobody who has not seen them can ever understand...You may ask any one of them, any moment of the day or night, 'Are you cold?' or 'Are you wet?' – and you will get but one answer...always with a smile – 'Not too cold, sir' or 'Not too wet, sir'. It makes me feel sick.

While waiting for the order to advance, a young officer gives some final instructions to his men.

Even in death, many officer's thoughts were for those with whom they had shared so much. Vere Harmsworth, of the Royal Naval Division, wrote a letter in which he left all his possessions for 'the men of my Battalion. My whole being is bound up with my men, heart, body and soul. Nothing else seems to matter.' Lieutenant Lucquiard, of the 68th Infantry Regiment, was hit by a shell burst in May 1915. A Private Poupiard carried him back to the trench. Lucquiard wrote out his will in a notebook: 'My thanks to all those who have fought with me, you must tell my parents that I always did my duty.' As a final postscript he managed to scrawl: 'You must not attempt to carry me back because the Bosch are going to take the trench. 500 francs of my money for Poupiard.' Then he died.

There are countless examples of the general sense of comradeship that affected all fighting soldiers on the Western Front. The love was both general and particular. Friendships were forged there that had no real parallel in civilian life. A Frenchman, A. Pezard, wrote: 'I can only speak of those times when we were friends among friends. Much will be forgiven this war because of the friendships that were formed there and the joy of being friends.' An English soldier tried to describe the deep friendships that grew up between men at the front and the reaction to the ever present likelihood of their suddenly being sundered: 'The love that grows quickly and perhaps artificially when men are together up against life and death has a peculiar quality. Death that cuts it off does not touch the emotions at all, but works right in the soul of you.' Certainly, for many soldiers, the loss of one's friends was one of the worst tortures of the war. Greenwell wrote bitterly of the death of two fellow-officers in May 1915: 'Funny that they couldn't leave even one of my two best friends.' Lieutenant St. Leger of the 2nd Coldstream Guards wrote of his friends who had fallen, trying to convince himself that one day they would be reunited, that such a great love could not simply disappear into the void:

> But meantime Denis, Henry and all those others are happy together – supremely happy...and they are waiting for me to join them and when I do will give me a great welcome. Then I will understand everything and be happy and content...Nothing can recall the past, so it is no use worrying or being unhappy about it. But I feel I have lost interest in everything.

But it was not simply the love of close friends that sustained men. Had this been so, their loss might have broken many men completely. There was a deep affection for everyone that had to endure the same horrors, an uplifting sense of unity and of pride in one's own and one's fellows' ability to stand

'Do you remember how it was down under'. Australian engineers resting in the vaults beneath the ramparts of Ypres.

firm in the midst of hell itself. Compassion and pride came together to form a brotherhood of the damned. Sydney Rogerson wrote after the war that those years 'will stand out in the memories of vast numbers of those who fought as the happiest period of their lives...In spite of all the differences in rank, we were comrades, brothers, dwelling together in unity'. A Frenchman, H. Malheabe, made a very similar point: 'Without regard to rank or social station, we were profoundly attached one to the other. Under the undeserved bleakness of our destiny, we felt a sense of brotherhood with our comrades in combat which death itself could not obliterate.' A private soldier wrote:

> To live amongst men who would give their last fag, their last bite, aye, even their last breath if need be for a pal – that is comradeship, the comradeship of the trenches. The only clean thing borne of this life of cruelty and filth. It grows in purity from the very obscenity of its surroundings.

Yet there is something rather frightening in this shared love because it sprang from such a sense of alienation. The soldiers' increasing estrangement from the home front was the darker side of their own comradeship, in that they could only feel at home with the men in the trenches. Frederick Manning movingly conveyed the desperate impulses behind the soldiers' mutual love:

> These apparently rude and brutal natures comforted, encouraged and reconciled each other to fate, with a tenderness and tact which was more moving than anything in life. They had nothing; not even their own bodies, which had become mere implements of warfare. The turned from the wreckage and misery of life to an empty heaven, and from an empty heaven to the silence of their own hearts. They had been brought to the last extremity of hope, and yet they put their hands on each others' shoulders and said with a passionate conviction that it would be all right, though they had faith in nothing, but in themselves and in each other.

Many men felt an irresistible pull to go back to the trenches, even as they realised how appalling were the conditions. A German soldier, Helmut Zschulte, wrote just before his death in late 1917:

> I am restless. I hate the kitchen table at which I am writing. I lost patience over a book. I should like to push the landscape aside as if it irritated me. I must get to the Front. I must again hear the shells roaring up into the sky and the desolate valley echoing the sound. I must get back to my Company...live once more in the realm of death.

Siegfried Sasoon described his sense of frustration and guilt whilst in England on sick leave. In one poem called 'Sick Leave' he wrote:

In bitter safety I awake, unfriended;
And while the dawn begins with slashing rain
I think of the Battalion in the mud.
'When are you going out to them again?
Are they not still your brothers through our blood?'

The fitting room. Ex-combatants waiting to exercise their artificial limbs.

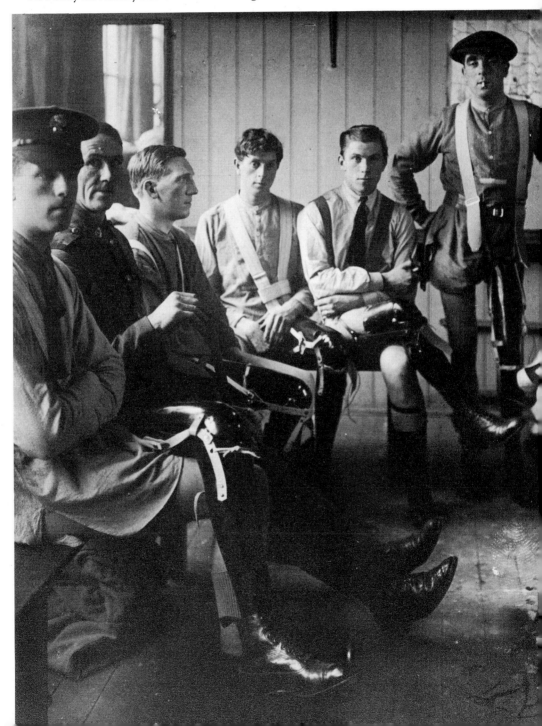

One of the most passionate statements of this sense of solidarity was made by Wilfred Owen in the 'Apologia Pro Poemate Meo':

> I have made fellowships –
>   Untold of happy lovers in old song.
>   For love is not the binding of fair lips
>   With the soft silk of eyes that look and long,
>
> By Joy, whose ribbon slips –
>   But wound with war's hard wire whose stakes are strong;
>   Bound with the bandage of the arm that drips;
>   Knit in the webbing of the rifle thong.

Yet he ends the poem by expressing his sense of complete isolation, of exclusivity, of contempt, even, for those who have not shared the ordeal:

> Nevertheless, except you share
>   With them in hell the sorrowful dark of hell,
>   Whose world is but the trembling of a flare,
>   And heaven but as the highway for a shell,
>
> You shall not hear their mirth:
>   You shall not come to think them well content
>   By any jest of mine. These men are worth
>   Your tears. You are not worth their merriment.

But no matter how moving, how uplifting one finds this passionate sense of brotherhood, the war in the trenches was one of unparallelled brutality and suffering. The First World War produced countless heroes and acts of love and self-sacrifice. Its literature is inspirational in its portrayal of love, compassion, courage and the capacity to endure. Yet all these men would have died for nothing if one did not also insist that the Western Front was an unparallelled nightmare of filth, decay, noise, blood and death, in which men fought for reasons they hardly understood, for a future they almost ceased to believe in, and which offered nothing when it came. Ezra Pound wrote an epitaph for those men much more suitable than the misty-eyed sentimentality of Remembrance Day:

> Died some, pro patria,
>   non 'dulce' non 'et decor'...Walked eye-deep in hell
> believing in old men's lies, then unbelieving
> came home, home to a lie,
> home to many deceits,
> home to old lies and new infamy.

Mourn, certainly, for those who fell, but remember men
moaning and weeping in an artillery barrage, men gibbering
in a shell-shock ward, men drowning in the mud, men fixedly
concentrating on holding their guts in their ripped bodies.
There are two images that sum up the ghastly futility of the
Great War. One is the picture of a soldier going out on a raid,
all identification removed, crawling out into the utter
blackness to grapple with an enemy he has hardly ever seen –
the nameless sent forth to kill the faceless. The other is the net
result of all the rhetoric about 'Homes fit for Heroes', the
choice of the Unknown Warrior. A blindfolded 'British officer
of very high rank' was guided into a hut containing the
remains of six bodies, taken from the various salients. The first
coffin he touched as he groped about was taken back to
Westminster Abbey to be buried with full military honours.
Then, one hopes, the general finally removed his blindfold.

SUGGESTIONS FOR FURTHER READING

Anyone wishing to get some impression of the vast amount of material available need only look in the subject catalogue of a large library, where it soon becomes apparent that books of the Great War were a staple of British publishing in the 1920s and 1930s. The suggestions below are but a drop in the ocean, and indeed only a fraction of the works consulted in the preparation of this book.

The best history of the war as a whole is B. Liddell Hart, *History of the First World War,* Pan Books, London, 1970.

Good books on individual years and campaigns are A. Clark, *The Donkeys,* Hutchinson, London, 1961; A. Horne, *The Price of Glory,* Macmillan, London, 1962; M. Middlebrook, *The First Day of the Somme,* Allen Lane, London, 1970; A. McKee, *Vimy Ridge,* Souvenir Press, London, 1966; L. Wolff, *In Flanders Fields,* Longmans, London, 1959; B. Pitt, *3918: The Last Act,* Cassell, London, 1962.

The best eye-witness accounts include S. Rogerson, *Twelve Days,* A. Barker, London, 1931; F.C. Hitchcock, *Stand To,* Hurst and Blackett, London, 1937; C. Carrington, *Soldier From the Wars Returning,* Hutchinson, London, 1965; F.P. Crozier, *A Brass Hat in No Man's Land,* Cape, London, 1930. Good anthologies are G. Chapman (ed.), *Vain Glory,* Cassell, London, 1937; G. Panichas (ed.), *Promise of Greatness,* Cassell, London, 1968; C.B. Purdom, *Everyman at War,* Dent, London, 1930; Anon., *Fifty Amazing Stories of the Great War,* Odhams Press, London, 1936. Of the novels see S. Sassoon, *Memoirs of an Infantry Officer,* Cassell, London, 1932; H. Williamson, *The Patriot's Progress,* G. Bles, London, 1930; F. Manning, *Her Privates We,* P. Davies, London, 1930; H. Barbusse, *Under Fire,* Dent, London, 1933. A good collection of poetry can be found in I.M. Parsons, *Men Who March Away,* Heinemann, London, 1968; though A.S.J. Adcock's collection *For Remembrance,* Hodder and Stoughton, London, 1918, is perhaps more typical of the period. On the literature of the First World War see P. Fussell, *The Great War and Modern Memory,* Oxford University Press, London, 1985.

Other illuminating books on the war from the soldiers' point of view are J. Brophy and E. Partridge, *The Long Trial,* Sphere Books, London, 1969; J. Baynes, *Morale,* Cassell, London, 1967. For the French see above all J. Meyer, *La vie quotidienne des soldats pendant la grande guerre,* Hachette, Paris, 1966. For the Americans see L. Stallings, *The Doughboys,* Harper and Row, New York, 1963.

Index

not made in straight lines 14-15;
conditions in 44-59; sanitation
arrangements in 52-3; vermin in
54-8
Troyte-Bullock, Colonel 45
Truces, 170-3
Tyndale-Biscoe, Julian 119

Unknown Warrior, choice of 205
Unreality, experienced in battle
100-4

Vauban, Marshal 12
Vegetables 125
Venereal diseases 153; punishments
for 154-5
Verdun 30, 37, 97
Vermin 54-8
Vernède, R.E. 140
Vimy Ridge 64, 130
Vosges 31

Walker, Reverend 114
War Office 57, 196
Warfare 3
Water 130-1; effect of in trenches
44-8

Weapons, used in trench raids 77-9
Weather conditions, effect on trench
life 44-53
Weil's Disease 55
West, Arthur Graeme 72, 75, 98,
176-7
Western Front 52, 59, 102, 106,
172, 190, 196, 204
Whale-oil 49
Wilkinson, Spencer 85
Williamson, Henry 119-20, 180
Wilson, Captain T.C. 176
'Winkle raids' 76
Winter 51
Wire 24-5
Wiring parties 24-5, 74
Working party 40
Wounds, kinds 109; *see also* Casualties
Wytshaete-Messines Ridge 10

YMCA 148
Ypres 10, 45
Ypres Salient 24, 44

Zones 20-1, 22-4
Zschulte, Helmut 202